China's Modern Economic Statecraft

This compelling exploration delves into President Xi Jinping's ambitious efforts to restore China to its historical role as a global leader through innovative economic means. Bridging the philosophies of Mao Zedong and Deng Xiaoping, Xi's approach is a unique synthesis of Marxist-Developmentalist ideas, aiming to convert China's accumulated national wealth into great power status.

At the heart of this narrative is a wealth-power dialectic, shaping the performance and challenges of China's modern economic statecraft. The book chronicles the optimism of Xi's first term, the overreach and subsequent retrenchment of his second, all set against the backdrop of a slowing domestic economy and intensifying strategic competition with the United States. Despite these hurdles, the Chinese government continues to expand its arsenal of economic tools and initiatives, showcasing resilience and adaptability.

This book offers an insightful look into how Xi Jinping's tenure might be remembered as a pinnacle in China's Marxist-Developmentalist economic history. This book is a must-read for anyone interested in understanding the intricate strategies behind China's quest for global preeminence.

Zhang Xiaotong is a professor in the Department of Political Science and International Relations and Director of the China and Central Asia Studies Center at KIMEP University, Kazakhstan. He obtained his PhD in political science from the Université Libre de Bruxelles (ULB) in Belgium.

Routledge Studies in the Modern World Economy

The Governance of Economic Development
Investment, Innovation, and Competition in China
Anson Au

The Economics of Russia's War in Ukraine
Impact Analysis of Economic Policy and Finance
Nataliya Struk, Maryana Prokop and Oleksandra Struk

Cybersecurity, Law and Economics
The Case of India
Edited by Dr. Gagandeep Kaur, Dr. Narendra N. Dalei, Dr. Sushanta Kumar Mahapatra and Dr. Vinay Kandpal

International Economic Policy for the Polycrisis
Edited by Konrad Raczkowski and Piotr Komorowski

Mega-Regional Trade Agreements and India
Balancing Economic and Strategic Concerns
Pankhuri Gaur

Wealth-Power Dialectic
China's New Economic Statecraft
Zhang Xiaotong

Sustainable Health Promotion Practices and the Global Economy
Edited by Ben Y.F. Fong and Wang-Kin Chiu

For more information about this series, please visit: www.routledge.com/Routledge-Studies-in-the-Modern-World-Economy/book-series/SE0432

China's Modern Economic Statecraft

A Wealth-Power Dialectic

Zhang Xiaotong

Routledge
Taylor & Francis Group
LONDON AND NEW YORK

First published 2025
by Routledge
4 Park Square, Milton Park, Abingdon, Oxon OX14 4RN

and by Routledge
605 Third Avenue, New York, NY 10158

Routledge is an imprint of the Taylor & Francis Group, an informa business

British Library Cataloguing-in-Publication Data
A catalogue record for this book is available from the British Library

Library of Congress Cataloging-in-Publication Data
Names: Zhang, Xiaotong (College teacher), author.
Title: China's modern economic statecraft : a wealth-power dialectic / Zhang Xiaotong.
Description: Abingdon, Oxon ; New York, NY : Routledge, 2025. | Series: Routledge studies in the modern world economy | Includes bibliographical references and index.
Identifiers: LCCN 2024033831 | ISBN 9781032218700 (hardback) | ISBN 9781032218717 (paperback) | ISBN 9781003270379 (ebk)
Subjects: LCSH: China--Economic policy--2000- | China--Economic conditions--2000-
Classification: LCC HC427.95 .Z435286 2025 |
DDC 330.951--dc23/eng/20240828
LC record available at https://lccn.loc.gov/2024033831

ISBN: 9781032218700 (hbk)
ISBN: 9781032218717 (pbk)
ISBN: 9781003270379 (ebk)

DOI: 10.4324/9781003270379

Typeset in Times New Roman
by KnowledgeWorks Global Ltd.

Contents

List of Tables

Abstract

President Xi is practicing what might be termed "Major-Country Economic Statecraft with Chinese Characteristics". At its core, this approach aims to restore China to its "natural" historical role as a global leader through economic means. However, Xi's philosophy of economic statecraft represents more continuity than change from the traditional economic statecraft of Mao Zedong to Deng Xiaoping. We describe Xi's approach as a synthesis of Marxist-Developmentalist philosophies. To achieve China's "great rejuvenation", China's economic statecraft aims to convert the national wealth accumulated over the past 40 years into great power status. This new economic statecraft, born from frustration with President Hu's low-profile diplomacy, has faced domestic constraints due to significant deceleration in China's economy, along with global challenges, particularly strategic competition with the United States. A wealth-power dialectic underpins the performance of China's economic statecraft. During Xi's tenure, his economic statecraft was marked by optimism in his first term, followed by overreach and subsequent retrenchment in his second term and beyond. As China confronts an increasingly challenging international environment, the Chinese government is rapidly expanding its arsenal of economic statecraft with new initiatives and legal tools, demonstrating resilience in its economic strategies.

Acknowledgments

This book can be seen as a continuation and extension of my previous work, "New Economic Statecraft: China, the USA, and the EU" (Zhang, 2023). As the world enters a turbulent period, economic statecraft has emerged as a major research subject and policy tool for major countries, becoming a key area of competition.

I have been researching economic statecraft for ten years. The concept first caught my attention during a speech by former US Secretary of State Hillary Clinton. She stated, "Economic statecraft has two parts: first, how we harness the forces and use the tools of global economics to strengthen our diplomacy and presence abroad; and second, how we put that diplomacy and presence to work to strengthen our economy at home" (Clinton, 2011). Her definition, which sees economic statecraft as a two-way conversion between wealth and power, resonates well with China's approach, particularly its focus on economic development (wealth creation) and the use of economic strengths to exert global influence (converting wealth to power).

During my tenure at the US Desk of the Chinese Ministry of Commerce, China and the United States managed their bilateral relationship through two major economic statecraft platforms – the US-China Joint Commission on Commerce and Trade (JCCT) and the US-China Strategic and Economic Dialogue (S&ED). Unfortunately, these platforms ceased to function after Donald Trump became President of the United States in 2017, a significant loss. Since then, we have witnessed an increase in negative economic statecraft, exemplified by the US-China Trade War in 2018.

The impetus for writing this book, *China's Modern Economic Statecraft*, was President Xi Jinping's implementation of a proactive economic statecraft with Chinese characteristics, exemplified by the Belt and Road Initiative. As I delved deeper, I found it necessary to include chapters on China's classical economic statecraft based on Confucian philosophy since Xi's strategies were inspired by Confucianism. The more I wrote, the more I realized that Xi Jinping's economic statecraft is a continuation and synthesis of the strategies of previous leaders from Mao Zedong to Deng Xiaoping, making it essential to consider this continuum rather than isolating Xi Jinping's strategies.

I also added a subtitle for this book, "A Wealth-Power Dialectic", as it is key to understanding the opportunities and challenges of China's economic statecraft. The success or failure of this statecraft is largely determined by the management of the wealth-power dialectic. An equilibrium exists between wealth and power. The key to maintaining this equilibrium is to promote economic growth and avoid overstretching.

This book is not a theoretical discourse removed from reality; it reflects the broader context since 2008. Having been both a practitioner and now an academic, I have experienced, observed, and researched these major events. Xi Jinping's economic statecraft, however, was the catalyst for my decision to write this book. In China's case, economic statecraft is a wealth-power conversion process deeply rooted in the country's unique history, contemporary challenges, and the pressures of great power competition. This book provides a classic Chinese perspective, highlighting ancient thoughts and practices of economic statecraft.

This book originated from my article published in The Washington Quarterly. I would like to thank Alexander Lennon, Editor-in-Chief of The Washington Quarterly, who published my article "From Wealth to Power: China's New Economic Statecraft" in 2017, coauthored with Ambassador James Keith.

I would also like to thank Andrew Mertha, who kindly hosted me at the School of Advanced International Studies, Johns Hopkins University, during my sabbatical in 2023. This visit allowed me to focus on writing this book and provided opportunities to discuss economic statecraft with colleagues in the United States, including David Baldwin, Colin Flint, Paul Sharp, and Christina Davis. I give my special thanks to Pieter Bottelier, who has consistently encouraged me to deliver this book. I owe him a great deal of gratitude.

Finally, I give my deepest thanks to my family – my parents, my wife, and my two adorable daughters. This book is for them. They give me love and unreserved support.

Zhang Xiaotong
Almaty, Kazakhstan
April 23, 2024

Reference List

Clinton, H. (2011) *Economic Statecraft Speech.* Economic Club of New York, New York.

Zhang, X. T. (2023) *New Economic Statecraft: China, the United States and the European Union.* Oxford: Taylor & Francis.

Introduction

China's New Economic Statecraft in the Making

Xi Jinping has championed China's new economic statecraft, which can be described as "major-country economic statecraft with Chinese characteristics". This approach is exemplified by many ambitious projects, including the Belt and Road Initiative (BRI), the Asian Infrastructure Investment Bank (AIIB), and Bilateral Investment Treaties (BITs) with the United States and the EU. Xi is the first Chinese leader since Mao Zedong who is keen on leveraging China's accumulated national wealth to enhance its prominent position on the world stage.

However, China's journey toward its new economic statecraft began before Xi Jinping came into office. In many ways, the year 2008, marked by the Global Financial Crisis, was a turning point. This period significantly boosted China's confidence in asserting itself on the global stage, particularly in the realm of global economic governance. On October 9, 2012, China's Ministry of Foreign Affairs set up the Department of International Economic Affairs. On April 1, 2014, China's Minister of Commerce, Mr. Gao Hucheng, published a policy commentary in the journal *Qiushi*, titled "Let the Chinese Dream Lighten a Beautiful World: Learning and Implementing General Secretary Xi Jinping's Thoughts on Economic Diplomacy", calling for learning and adoption of the Xi Jinping's thoughts on economic diplomacy (Gao, 2014).

Beginning around 2013, when Xi Jinping assumed office, China's policy and academic community initiated a debate regarding the nation's "great power economic statecraft" (in China's narrative, often called "Major Country Economic Diplomacy", "大国经济外交" in Chinese). This debate focused on three key questions: First, what defines major country economic statecraft, and what are its main characteristics? Second, does China's economic statecraft qualify as major country economic statecraft, and in what ways does it differ from or resemble the economic statecraft of other major countries? Third, how can China advance its unique form of economic statecraft? This policy debate was not strictly top-down; rather, it was a combination of both top-down and bottom-up approaches. There was a converging consensus among Chinese policy elites and the academic community that some changes needed to be made with the advent of a new leader and as China's national

DOI: 10.4324/9781003270379-1

wealth had accumulated to an extent that it needed to be wielded more effectively to enhance China's global influence.

0.1 The Concept of "Major Country Economic Diplomacy"

Since President Xi Jinping began implementing "Major Country Diplomacy with Chinese Characteristics" in 2013, the concept of "major country economic diplomacy" was accordingly developed and implemented. "Major country economic diplomacy" is, in simple terms, economic diplomacy as practiced by major countries (or great powers). Specifically, it refers to the act, art, and process of wealth-power conversion by a great power to realize and maintain its status as such.[1] Great power economic diplomacy is generally characterized by three main features: the might, the will, and the influence of a great power.[2] Below is a detailed explanation of these three main features of great power economic diplomacy, through which we can assess whether Xi's China is practicing so-called great power economic diplomacy.

First, the might of a great power. A great power is a country that is militarily and economically powerful, particularly its military might. A great power can wield substantial power resources in the exercise of economic diplomacy. It has strategic latitude and room for power maneuvers to impose or counter sanctions. But the reality of international relations is that no country is "all-mighty" in all areas of power. Even the United States is not an "all-round champion" with power resources in all sectors. The United States enjoys global supremacy in military power, but not in the economic field. Therefore, a measure of a great power is also its ability to channel power resources across fields, as well as the degree and efficiency of the mutual transformation of power resources from different sources. Robert Keohane and Joseph Nye, in their book *Power and Interdependence*, address this issue by saying: "Militarily and economically, states will dominate a variety of organizations and a variety of issues by linking their own policies on some issues to other states' policies on other issues. By using their overall dominance to prevail on their weak issues, the strongest states will, in the traditional model, ensure a congruence between the overall structure of military and economic power and the pattern of outcomes on any one issue area. Thus, world politics can be treated as a seamless web" (Keohan and Nye, 2002). The underlying message is that great powers can link issues to redeploy power resources from one issue area to another, thereby ensuring their dominance in a particular area of interest. The author argues that great power economic diplomacy involves frequent political and economic interactions, and therefore, economic diplomacy can be defined as, "the two-way conversion between wealth and power" (Zhang, 2013).

Second, the will of a great power. Apart from economic interests, major countries have strategic interests, political ambitions, and a strong sense of strategic planning. Economic diplomacy is "the act, art, and process of transforming wealth and power mutually through strategy, tactics, and institutional design by a national government in its external relations" (Zhang, 2013). It emphasizes initiative and long-term planning. Generally, based on its own strong wealth base and motivated by its ambitions and goals, a great power has strong demand for the two-way transformation of wealth and power, and therefore, a stronger will for such transformation than the medium- and small-sized countries. The intensity, speed, and scale of such transformation are much higher in a great power than in a small nation or a middle power. All these require the great power to plan ahead and craft forward-looking economic diplomacy. Emerging powers, on the other hand, must catch up with the established powers. For example, the United States caught up with Britain in the late 19th to mid-20th centuries, and Japan caught up with the United States in the 1970s and 1980s. Conversely, incumbent powers use all available resources to curb rising powers. As great power status is a scarce resource, competition for such status is conceivably intense. The final result is often that one will be the loser, worse-off, and in a more suppressed position than before (Zhang, 2007). Thus, great power economic diplomacy must follow the political ambitions of the great power. Great power economic diplomacy is essentially about serving the strategic interests of the great power through economic statecraft, and the strategic interests of a great power lie in pursuing its goals, participating in the power shift in the international system, and actively shaping the world order.

Third, the influence of a great power. Great powers usually have influence beyond their own regions. Barry Buzan, an American scholar, suggests that the influence of a great power can span more than one region, and the influence of a superpower can extend to the entire international system (Buzan, 2011). Therefore, great power economic diplomacy emphasizes the acquisition of trans-regional influence, discourse power, control, and decision power. At present, the economic diplomacy of the United States, the EU,[3] and China all contain a global perspective and global influence. Notwithstanding the impact of the global financial crisis, US economic diplomacy still maintains a global footprint. It advanced the negotiations of the Trans-Pacific Partnership (TPP) in the Asia-Pacific region, which was later canceled by President Donald Trump. The United States also diplomatically intervened in the Russia-Ukraine conflict in Eurasia, imposing economic sanctions on Russia, and consolidated its role in NATO for transatlantic relations. Additionally, it negotiated the Transatlantic Trade and Investment Partnership (TTIP) agreement with the European Union, which was again canceled by President Trump. Following the adoption of the Lisbon Treaty, the EU established the European External Action Service (EEAS) and proposed ten strategic partnerships to strengthen ties with other major powers and emerging economies. The EU actively pursued regionalism, exemplified by the US-EU Transatlantic Free Trade Agreement negotiations, and strengthened its economic ties with emerging economies in Asia. During this period, China's economic diplomacy progressed from a focus on domestic ("interior line") to international ("exterior line") affairs, expanding its influence to Africa, Latin America, and Europe.

In summary, great power economic diplomacy is characterized by being guided by the ambitions of a great power. It is based on the strength of such powers and driven by the primary aim of acquiring or maintaining their status as great powers. The strategic goal of great power economic diplomacy is achieved through transforming national wealth into international power and influence, rather than vice versa.

0.2 China's Major Country Economic Statecraft in the Making

During President Hu Jintao's tenure (2002–2012), China's status as a major country was without serious dispute, but the extent to which China's economic statecraft conformed to the model of great power economic statecraft defined above remains open to discussion. In the author's view, China's economic statecraft before Xi Jinping had the strength of a great power and practiced wealth-power transformation on a large scale and across sectors, along with a certain degree of international influence. However, it lacked a key element: the core objectives of great power economic statecraft. One must question whether the primary objective of China's economic diplomacy was focused on power transition among great powers and shaping the international political and economic order, or on domestic economic and social development. During Hu Jintao's tenure, the Chinese official statements suggested that the primary goal of China's economic diplomacy was domestic economic and social development, paving the way for a comprehensive deepening of domestic reforms (Wang, 2013b). In this sense, prior to Xi Jinping's leadership, China had not yet demonstrated the policy or strategic readiness for implementing great power economic statecraft and lacked the strong will and clear ambitions characteristic of a great power. However, under Xi Jinping's leadership, there was a significant shift, with a growing emphasis on the core objective of China's major-country economic statecraft being to foster power transition and to build a new international order. Thus, Xi Jinping's approach to economic statecraft is closer to what can be qualified as "great power economic statecraft", but it is not there yet.

When Xi Jinping took over China's statecraft from Hu Jintao, he inherited both advantages and challenges in cultivating a true sense of great power economic statecraft. Over time, these elements played out and had various effects on Xi Jinping's ambition to move China to the center of the world stage.

0.2.1 China's Current National Conditions and Stage of Development

When implementing economic statecraft, China must consider its current stage of development, national conditions, and public opinion. Xi Jinping is no exception. To a large extent, the primary goal of the Chinese government's economic statecraft remains to serve China's economic and social development and to improve people's living standards since 1978, when China started reform and opening-up. On the principles of China's economic diplomacy, the then Chinese Commerce Minister Gao Hucheng argued in 2014 that "we must adhere to the strategic policy of having diplomacy serve economic goals" (Gao, 2014).

During Xi Jinping's first term (2012–2017), China's major economic diplomacy initiatives, such as the BRI, high-speed rail diplomacy, and nuclear energy diplomacy, were all closely linked to domestic development. The land-based Silk Road Economic Belt was designed to develop the western region (especially Xinjiang) and to redress the current imbalance in development between the eastern and western regions. The Bangladesh-China-India-Myanmar (BCIM) Economic Corridor and the China-Pakistan Economic Corridor (CPEC) are aimed at developing China's southwestern region, improving the region's transportation and communication infrastructure, stimulating economic development in the border areas, narrowing the development gap across regions, and enhancing border defense. High-speed rail diplomacy aims to export the excess domestic manufacturing capacity of high-speed rail. China has high expectations for the high-speed rail in improving national modernization, technology sophistication, economic strength, international competitiveness, and independent innovation capacity and has vigorously invested in the sector. As a result, the mileage of high-speed railroads built by China in under a decade has exceeded that of newly-built high-speed railways by developed countries in the West over the past 50 years. The excess capacity made it imperative for China to adopt high-speed rail diplomacy and to export its highly-scaled high-speed rail technology and manufacturing capacity.

This is evidence of a dual purpose in China's economic statecraft, which shifts between economic development and the attainment of strategic goals as a great power, with the former being the central objective. This is necessitated by China's basic national conditions of still being a developing country at the primary stage of socialism. In great power economic statecraft, economic and political interactions and wealth-power transformation are often at odds. When economic strength is a given factor, having the economy serve politics will likely affect economic growth. Conversely, having politics serve the economy can undermine the pursuit of great power status. In fact, for a long time, China's economic diplomacy prioritized serving the domestic economy, with its primary goal being to foster economic and social development at home. Going forward, it remains to be seen whether the primary goal of China's economic diplomacy will pivot to using economic strengths to pursue international power status. Despite Xi Jinping's leadership, this approach has not fundamentally changed, as China has not yet achieved the status of a fully developed country. In fact, after Xi came into power, China's economy slowed down, necessitating a focus on domestic economic and social development over competing for global leadership in its economic diplomacy.

0.2.2 China's Regime Characteristics

The strong leadership of the Communist Party of China (CPC) and its efficient and powerful government are conducive to the implementation of great power economic statecraft. This is the second feature of China's economic statecraft. In stark contrast to China, the US government has experienced repeated "shutdowns" due to budgetary constraints. Due to bipartisan disagreements in Congress, the fast-track authority for brokering trade deals has been terminated, which seriously undermined the credibility of the United States in TPP and TTIP negotiations. The IMF reform bill was also repeatedly shelved by Congress.[4] All of these have greatly set back the international influence of the United States. The US system is known for the separation of powers, partisan fighting, and congressional constraints. From historical experience, a strong US executive and a weak Congress would make strong US economic diplomacy. On the contrary, a strong Congress and a weak executive will constrict its economic diplomacy. American scholar Fareed Zakaria found that the United States did not proactively transform its wealth into international influence during the 1865–1889 period when its economic power was rising rapidly. Instead, the United States adopted aggressive foreign diplomacy and rapidly expanded its overseas interests during 1889–1908. Why? Zakaria's explanation is that the growth of government power and the realization by key policymakers of the relative strength of government power were the main reasons why the United States moved from under-expansion to active expansion. This is thought-provoking and helps us to better recognize the regime characteristics of China's economic statecraft – the strong leadership of the CPC, active state leadership, and an efficient and assertive government. This is an important reason for the notable progress of China's economic statecraft. Since Xi Jinping took office as General Secretary, China's diplomacy has taken on a new look of progressiveness and innovation, as Wang Yi, China's Foreign Minister proudly claimed (Wang, 2013c). During Xi's rule, China relied on its regime and institutional strengths to further improve top-level design and drive the implementation of economic statecraft. One significant feature of Xi's economic statecraft was that he placed the CPC in the driving seat, with the Party leading all aspects.

0.2.3 China's Civilizational Characteristics and Historical Depth

The foundation of China's economic diplomacy with its own characteristics includes Xi Jinping's "correct concept of righteousness and economic benefit", which advocates balancing righteousness and benefit in engagement with developing countries with greater weight on righteousness (Wang, 2013a). It also includes the commercial culture that values ethics over profit and cautions against profiteering and egoism (Gao, 2014). Zhang Qian's mission to the Western Regions led to the establishment of diplomatic ties between the Han Dynasty and the countries in the Western Regions and flourishing friendship along the ancient Silk Road. It also brought the civilization, knowledge, and products of the Western Regions back to China. In Chinese history, there were also Admiral Zheng He's seven voyages to the Western Ocean, which is today's Indian Ocean. These embodied the Confucian spirit of "accommodating people from afar, building harmony with all nations, and sharing peace around the world", and facilitating economic engagement and commodity trade. This contrasts sharply with the slave trade and colonial rule by the Western powers through their powerful ships and cannons (Research Center of Economic Diplomacy, Wuhan University, 2014). China's distinctive civilizational identity and heritage have helped the country chart a path of economic diplomacy different from that of other great powers – to engage with other countries from a civilizational perspective and to carry out major-country economic diplomacy more effectively.

0.3 Major Challenges Preventing China from Practicing Great Power Economic Statecraft

In its transition to great power economic statecraft, China faced two major challenges during both Hu Jintao and Xi Jinping's tenures.

First, domestic constraints. The domestic interests of great powers are compound and multifaceted, and competing national objectives, friction, and constraints among different interest groups, power play among different government agencies, popular pressure, and the collision of different schools of thought may all contribute to the depletion of China's existing strengths. For example, civil society has increasingly become a major actor in China's economic diplomacy. At the apex of the European debt crisis, when Europe lacked liquidity, Wenzhou, a Chinese city, also plunged into a private sector credit crisis due to a lack of liquidity, and private enterprises went bankrupt. As to the question of whether China should bail out Europe or Wenzhou, public opinion was overwhelmingly in favor of Wenzhou (Bai, 2011), which added to the complexity of decision-making by the Chinese leadership. China's aid to Macedonia's school bus project, a routine aid operation, also triggered heated discussions on the internet. One user said, "I am not against helping others, but I can't stand that our own schoolchildren are riding in scrapped buses and seriously overloaded vans!" (Phoenix Info, 2011) These civil pressures have raised a new question for the government: will foreign diplomacy and internal affairs become incongruent, and which should come first? Regardless of the answer, the current debate itself has already placed constraints on the external projection of China's economic power.

Second, overstretch and depletion of power resources. Historical experience suggests that squandering power resources will lead to the decline of great powers. According to Paul Kennedy, the decline of a great power is the result of military overexpansion and lack of financial resources. Strategic overexpansion (e.g., encroaching on large territories and expensive wars) can lead to the decline of a great power (Kennedy, 2013). There is a limit to the transformation of wealth into power; over-expenditure of wealth and militarization will invite the decline of the state. The American political scientist Jack Snyder, in his book *Myths of Empire*, also mentions that empires often have the myth that national security can only be preserved by over-expansion. This notion is the main driver behind the over-expansion of all the industrialized powers, yet it is precisely this aggressive policy that has undermined national security (Snyder, 2007). The main reason why over-expansion undermines national security and interests is the inefficient conversion between wealth and power, wasting too much wealth without acquiring the expected power. The collapse of the Soviet Union was largely due to its insufficient economic base to support diplomatic, strategic, and military expansion. It was a failure of Soviet economic statecraft and a triumph of American economic statecraft. Therefore, in economic statecraft practices, the efficiency of wealth-power conversion is critical to the rise and fall of great powers. The history of the rise and fall of great powers has repeatedly demonstrated that overconsumption of wealth and militarization will lead to the decline of national power. Xi Jinping's economic statecraft marks a significant departure from his predecessors and risks overstretching. Since he came to office, China's economy has started to slowdown. Consequently, there is a need for China to explore "smart ways" to transform wealth into power in an affordable and sustainable manner.

0.4 Structure of This Book

This book concentrates on China's economic statecraft during Xi Jinping's era. However, to fully comprehend Xi's approach, it is essential to explore the roots of China's economic statecraft in the classical age, specifically the Confucius-Mencius period. Further complicating this analysis is the fact that Xi's philosophy of economic statecraft represents more of a continuation than a break from the contemporary economic statecraft philosophy of Mao Zedong and Deng Xiaoping, which blends Marxist and Developmentalist ideas. In essence, Xi's economic statecraft can be seen as a synthesis: a Marxist-Developmentalist approach infused with insights from Confucius and Mencius.

This book is divided into five chapters. Chapter 1 delves into China's classical economic statecraft, examining the principles of Confucius and Mencius. Chapter 2 explores the post-1949 Economic Statecraft Model in China, characterized as Marxist-Developmentalist with Chinese Characteristics. Chapter 3 sheds light on Hu Jintao's economic statecraft (2002–2012), tracing the origins of China's new economic statecraft. Chapter 4 analyzes Xi Jinping's economic statecraft during his initial term from 2012 to 2017. Finally, Chapter 5 examines Xi's second term (2017–2022) and the initial two years of his third term (2022–2023), providing insights into the evolving nature of his economic strategies.

The Conclusion chapter finds that China's economic statecraft has evolved through three distinct approaches: (1) The approach of Emperor Zhu Di, who initiated Admiral Zheng He's voyages across the Indo-Pacific, symbolizing a period of exploration and maritime prowess. (2) Mao Zedong's approach, rooted in Marxist ideology and intertwined with China's classical history, representing a blend of ideological fervor and historical context. (3) Deng Xiaoping's approach, characterized by a developmentalist philosophy, focusing on economic growth and modernization as the primary drivers of statecraft. This chapter concludes that the remarkable economic ascent of China since 1978 can be attributed to a unique blend of Marxist ideology and developmentalist economics, a compromise forged within the CPC. This compromise maintained Marxism as the dominant ideological framework while simultaneously embracing economic liberalism as the driving force behind China's statecraft. However, the "Marxist-Developmentalist Compromise", a concept prevailing since Deng Xiaoping's era, is now being challenged. There is a growing risk of overextension in China's new economic statecraft, particularly in the context of China's economic slowdown and the Covid. Ultimately, the tension inherent in the conversion between wealth and power (wealth-power dialectic) remains one of the most significant challenges to China's rise. That is exactly why this book is titled *China's Modern Economic Statecraft: A Wealth-Power Dialectic*.

Notes

1 In the article "The Construction of a Theory on China's Economic Diplomacy: A Preliminary Attempt" (see Diplomatic Review, 2013, Issue 6), Zhang Xiaotong defines "economic diplomacy" as "the act, art, and process of a country's government subjectively and actively transforming wealth into power and vice versa through strategic, tactical, and institutional design in international interactions." Here, "wealth" refers to economic strength, economic resources (such as oil, raw materials, foreign exchange reserves, overseas investments, the strength of Chinese enterprises, etc.), economic means, and economic gains. "Power" refers to a position of advantage one party has over another, which can force the other party to accept its opinions and assertions and make them do things they originally did not want to do or had not planned to do. It is necessary to point out that power is not necessarily political or military power; it can also be economic power, cultural power, or power in any field. This book adopts this definition of economic diplomacy and provides a corresponding definition for "major-country economic diplomacy".

2 It is worth noting that in China's official narrative, "major country" is preferred over "great power", since the latter evokes associations with great power competition in the 19th century.

3 The European Union is a sovereign body composed of 27 sovereign states and plays an important role in the current multipolar context. After more than half a century of integration, the EU's main policy tools for economic diplomacy, such as trade policy, development aid, and enlargement, have largely become competencies of

the EU, implemented uniformly in foreign relations by the EU headquarters. For example, the European Commission is responsible for negotiating the "Transatlantic Trade and Investment Partnership Agreement" with the United States and bilateral investment treaty negotiations with China. At the same time, Eurozone countries implement a unified monetary policy and conduct unified financial diplomacy. In this context, we believe that the EU can be considered a group of great powers, and its economic diplomacy can be seen as that of a group of great powers. In fact, the EU's overall economic diplomacy is often stronger and more effective than that of general great powers. To better understand the economic diplomacy of great powers, we categorize the EU's economic diplomacy as a type of great power economic diplomacy.

4 On March 26, 2014, I attended a memorable debate in the United States. One side, consisting of the US government and the Democratic Party, proposed solving the International Monetary Fund (IMF)'s assistance to Ukraine and IMF quota reforms as a package deal. The other side, the Republican-controlled House of Representatives, opposed bundling IMF reform with the Ukrainian aid. Ultimately, the Democrats were forced to compromise, and the two issues were separated.

Reference List

Bai, M. (2011) *Save Europe First or Wenzhou first?*. 7 October. Available at: https://www.guancha.cn/indexnews/2011_10_08_60320.shtml

Buzan, B. (2011) "The Inaugural Kenneth N. Waltz Annual Lecture: A World Order without Superpowers: Decentered Globalism", *International Relations*. 25(3), p. 4.

Gao, H. C. (2014) *"Let the Chinese Dream Light up a Better World: Learning and Implementing Xi Jinping's Thoughts on Economic Diplomacy"* [Qiushi] 1 April.

Kennedy, P. (2013) "Introduction", *The Rise and Fall of Great Powers* (Part 1) (in Chinese). Beijing: Citic Press.

Keohan, R., and Nye, J. (2002) *Power and Interdependence* (in Chinese). Translated by Men, H. H. Beijing: Beijing University Press.

Phoenix Info. (2011) *"China's Free Aid to Macedonian School Buses Sparks Online Debate"* [Phoenix Info] 27 November. Available at: http://news.ifeng.com/mainland/special/gsyeyxiaochechehuo/content-3/detail_2011_11/27/10929244_0.shtml

Research Center of Economic Diplomacy, Wuhan University. (2014) *Advocating the 'Zheng He Spirit' and Implementing the 'Zheng He Initiative' to Vigorously Promote the Construction of the Maritime Silk Road.* April.

Snyder, J. (2007) *Myths of Empire* (in Chinese). Beijing: Beijing University Press.

Wang, Y. (2013a) *Exploring the Path of Major-country Diplomacy with Chinese Characteristics," Speech at the Luncheon of the Second World Peace Forum.* 27 June.

Wang, Y. (2013b) *Speech at the Symposium "New Starting Point, New Concept, New Practice: China and the World 2013"*. Available at: http://live.people.com.cn/note.php?id=357131213185739_ctdzb_004

Wang, Y. (2013c) *"The Successful Practice of Major-Country Diplomacy with Chinese Characteristics – Foreign Minister on China's Diplomacy in 2013"* [People's Daily] 19 December.

Zhang, X. J. (2007) *The Road to the Revival of Great Powers*. Beijing: People's Publishing House.

Zhang, X. T. (2013) "The Theoretical Framework of China's Economic Diplomacy: A Preliminary Attempt"(in Chinese)", *Foreign Affairs Review.* (6), p. 53.

1 China's Classic Economic Statecraft

Confucius-Mencius Philosophy

Economic statecraft, understood as the conversion of power into wealth, has been practiced by all dynasties and empires throughout human history. China is no exception; it has not only engaged in economic statecraft but also developed systematic theories of it over time.

China's prominent examples of economic statecraft practices include Zhang Qian's mission to the Western Regions (139 BCE–126 BCE), the Tributary System (202 BCE–19th century CE), and Admiral Zheng He's voyages (1405–1433 CE).

Historically, China's foreign policy largely relied on its economic supremacy. Ancient China's economy was the strongest in the world for a long stretch of time. In 1700, China's GDP accounted for 22.3% and in 1820, 32.9% of the world's total (Angus, 2007).

The ancient Chinese approach to economic statecraft significantly differed from the paradigms of Western great powers during modern times (1492 CE–1914 CE), such as mercantilism, liberalism, imperialism, or Marxism (Zhang, 2023, pp. 28–43). The core philosophy underpinning China's classical economic statecraft, rooted in Confucian ethics, focused not on profit but on morality and the sustenance of the Tributary System, which prevailed for over 2000 years (202 BCE to the end of the 19th century CE). In essence, ancient Chinese economic statecraft aimed at upholding a moral-based international order, reinforced through the Tributary System.

This chapter focuses on classic Chinese thoughts on economic statecraft and its historical practices (see Table 1.1), as well as its challenges.

1.1 Classic Chinese Thoughts on Statecraft – Confucius-Mencius Philosophy

"Statecraft" in Chinese is translated as "治国理政". In Chinese, "治国理政" (zhì guó lǐ zhèng) directly translates to "govern the country and manage politics". "治" (zhì) means "to govern" or "to rule". "国" (guó) refers to "country" or "nation". "理" (lǐ) means "to administer" or "to manage". "政" (zhèng) pertains to "politics" or "government".

DOI: 10.4324/9781003270379-2

Table 1.1 The Historical Evolution of China's Economic Statecraft

	Wealth	*China's economic statecraft* *Paradigm*	*Government*	*Power strategy*
202 BC–19th Century	Non-reciprocal trade, Admiral Zheng He's Voyages (1405–1433)	"Tianxia system" "Sous le ciel" Céleste Empire	Dynasties	Tributary system
1840–1911		Collapse of "Tianxia system", anti-imperialism, anti-colonialism	Qing Dynasty	Two Opium Wars (1839–1842, 1856–1860), The Taiping Heavenly Kingdom (1851–1864), Self-strengthening Movement (1861–1895), Sino-French War (1884–1885), the First Sino-Japanese War (1894–1895), the Hundred Days' Reform (1898), Boxer Rebellion (1899–1901), Eight-Nation Alliance (1900), The Wuchang Uprising, Fall of Qing Dynasty (1911)
1911–1949		Nationalism, anti-imperialism, anti-colonialism	Beiyang government (1913–1928), The Warlord Era (1916–1928), Nationalist government (1925–1948)	Yuan Shikai's failed attempt to restore monarchy (1915–1916), Manchu Restoration (1917), The May Fourth Movement (1919), Dr. Sun Yat-sen's "Three Principles of the People", Birth of Communist Party (1921), Northern Expedition (1926–1928), Anti-Japanese War (1931–1945), War of Liberation (1945–1949)

(Continued)

Table 1.1 (Continued)

	Wealth	*China's economic statecraft* *Paradigm*	*Government*	*Power strategy*
1949–1976	Marxism mixed with China's traditional way of thinking as a central kingdom	Marxism, anti-imperialism	Communist Mao Zedong	Korean War (1950–1953), "Leaning to One Side" (1949–1950s), Supporting Communist revolution, leading developing countries, support for a new international economic order, "Three Worlds" and "Middle Zone", Cultural Revolution (1966–1976)
1977–1992	Reform and opening-up, GATT accession	Socialism with Chinese Characteristics	Communist Deng Xiaoping	Deng Xiaoping Theory
1989–2002	GATT/WTO accession, building market economy with Chinese Characteristics	Socialism with Chinese Characteristics	Communist Jiang Zemin	"Three Represents"
2002–2012	Emerging strategic industries, indigenous innovation,	Socialism with Chinese Characteristics	Communist Hu Jintao	The Outlook of Scientific Development
2012–	"Silk Road Initiative" (BRI), Asia Infrastructure Investment Bank (AIIB), BRICS Development Bank; China's regionalism: RCEP, FTAAP; Domestic: Free Trade Zone; Supply-side reform; Community of Shared Destin; China International Development Cooperation Agency	Socialism with Chinese Characteristics	Communist Xi Jinping	Xi Jinping Thought on Socialism with Chinese Characteristics for a New Era

Source: Made by the author.

Put them together, statecraft ("治国理政") in Chinese is a term used to describe the art and science of governance, focusing on the principles and strategies of ruling a country and administering political affairs.

Throughout Chinese history, different dynasties and leaders have adopted and implemented various philosophies and strategies for statecraft. For instance, during the Zhou Dynasty (1046 BC–256 BC), the concept of the Mandate of Heaven was introduced, which served as a divine justification for the emperor's rule and established the moral obligations of the ruler toward his subjects. Similarly, during the Han Dynasty (202 BC–220 AD), Confucianism became the state ideology, emphasizing moral integrity, social harmony, and respect for tradition and authority in governance.

Confucius was an influential Chinese philosopher, teacher, and political theorist who lived between 551 and 479 BC. He is best known for his teachings on ethics, personal and governmental morality, and social relationships, which later formed the basis of Confucianism, a major philosophical and religious tradition in East Asia. Confucius emphasized the importance of family, respect for elders, and the cultivation of personal character and virtue in his teachings.

Confucius believed in the concept of the "Junzi" or "gentleman", which signifies a person of high moral character, righteousness, and benevolence. He also put forward the idea of the "Five Relationships", which include ruler-subject, father-son, husband-wife, elder brother-younger brother, and friend-friend, highlighting the significance of familial and social harmony. His teachings were later compiled in the "Analects", a collection of his sayings and ideas documented by his disciples.

Confucius' thoughts have profoundly influenced Chinese culture, society, and governance for over two millennia. His thoughts of statecraft were best captured in the phrase "修身" (self-cultivation), "齐家" (ordering the household), "治国" (governing the nation), "平天下" (bringing peace to the world) originating from the text "The Great Learning" (《大学》) written by Confucius and his disciples.[1] The progression illustrates the steps one should take to better oneself and subsequently make contributions to society and the nation.

Confucian diplomatic thought is derived from Confucian classics and teachings from later Confucian scholars. It emphasizes ritual, morality, peace, and harmony. The Confucian school advocates "Harmony without Uniformity" and "Harmonizing All Nations". Here are some core views of Confucian diplomatic thought:

1 Ritual and Etiquette: Confucianism believes that rituals are the cornerstone of maintaining social order and interpersonal relationships and are equally applicable to interactions between nations. Adhering to these rituals can ensure the harmony and stability of diplomatic relations.
2 Benevolence: Benevolence (Ren) is at the core of Confucian thought, signifying kindness and goodwill. Confucianism believes that interactions

between nations should be based on the principle of Ren, i.e., mutual respect, understanding, and care.

3 The Doctrine of the Mean: Confucianism advocates the middle path, which means avoiding extremes and seeking balance. In the diplomatic arena, this implies avoiding extreme strategies and actions and instead seeking peaceful and balanced solutions.
4 Harmony without Uniformity: This concept emphasizes seeking harmony while maintaining diversity. Even if two countries have cultural, political, or economic differences, they should seek common ground and coexist peacefully.
5 All under Heaven is for the Public: This idea promotes the shared interests and well-being between nations, rather than just pursuing the interests of one single country.
6 Harmonizing All Nations: Confucianism emphasizes that nations should live in peace with one another, rather than resolving disputes through war or violence.
7 Quality of Leadership: Confucianism believes that rulers or national leaders should possess noble moral qualities, which serve as a foundation for diplomacy. A morally upright leader is more likely to establish long-lasting and stable relationships with other nations.

In summary, Confucian diplomatic thought emphasizes morality, ritual, and peace. In foreign relations, there should be a pursuit of harmony, mutual respect, and shared interests.[2]

1.2 Confucius-Mencius Thoughts on Economic Statecraft

Confucius-Mencius thoughts on economic statecraft are best captured by Mencius' phrase "穷则独善其身，达则兼济天下" ("When impoverished, cultivate one's own moral character; when affluent, benefit the world"),[3] encapsulating the idea of a person's responsibility and behavior in different economic and social statuses. Simply put, the phrase suggests that when an individual has limited resources, they should focus on their own well-being and development; but when one has ample resources and capabilities, they should strive to help others and society.

Mencius' statement "When impoverished, cultivate one's own moral character; when affluent, benefit the world" is a philosophical and ethical idea that outlines the attitude and actions an individual or country should adopt when facing different circumstances. Literally, the saying speaks to the idea that one should focus on personal moral cultivation when in poverty or adversity; and when wealthy or influential, one should consider benefiting others or society as a whole.

This idea is somewhat related to China's economic statecraft. With its rapid economic growth, China has emerged as a major global economic power. This development positions the country to assume greater international responsibilities, including economic aid, investments, technology exchanges, and various forms of cooperation.

In this context, Mencius' notion can be understood as encouraging a country that has already become economically strong (like China) to consider not only its own interests in its foreign economic activities but also to consider cooperation and joint development with other countries and regions, aiming for a win-win situation.

Another key Confucius-Mencius concept of economic statecraft is called "Yi-Li" philosophy ("Yi" means moral while "Li" means benefit). The concept of "Yi-Li" generally refers to the viewpoint of weighing morality and benefits when making decisions. In traditional Confucian thought, especially in the teachings of Confucius and Mencius, there is indeed a distinction and discussion regarding "Yi" (morality) and "Li" (benefit).

Confucius emphasized that "Yi" should be placed before "Li". He believed that a noble person should prioritize morality rather than pursuing personal or short-term benefits. Confucius once said, "The noble person is aware of morality, the lesser person is aware of profit".[4] This implies that noble individuals should be guided by morality, while lesser individuals are guided by profit.

Mencius further developed this idea. He emphasized that human nature is fundamentally good and advocated nurturing this nature to achieve moral perfection. Mencius discussed with King Hui of Liang about attacking neighboring countries and insisted that if it could not be justified on moral grounds, then one should not attack neighboring countries for economic gain.

However, the teachings of Confucius and Mencius are not completely against pursuing benefits but oppose sacrificing morality to pursue benefits. In their view, the true benefit complements morality, that is, long-term and fair benefits will come with the practice of morality.

Mencius and King Hui of Liang had a discussion regarding the issue of morality versus profit. King Hui asked, "Is there a way to achieve the world?" Mencius replied, "There is; conquer it by war and one will achieve it, without enjoying war, one will not". The King asked, "Do I enjoy war?" Mencius answered, "You do not". The King queried further, to which Mencius elaborated, stating that true benefit for a country and its ruler comes from following the path of righteousness.[5] In this dialogue, Mencius revealed that pursuing profit while neglecting morality leads to long-term failure or harm, and real benefit is based on righteousness.

1.3 The Tribute System: China's Classic Institution of Economic Statecraft

The Tribute System represents a fundamental aspect of ancient East Asian international relations, serving as a pivotal diplomatic and economic institution throughout Chinese history. In essence, the Tribute System entailed subordinate states or regimes presenting tributes to a dominant central power, such as China, in exchange for reciprocation, protection, and recognition.

The origins of China's Tribute System trace back to ancient times, particularly the Zhou Dynasty era.

1 Western Zhou period: During this period, a preliminary form of the Tribute System emerged. Under feudalism, various vassal states needed to present tributes to the central authority of the Zhou Dynasty, as a sign of loyalty and respect. This system was mainly based on internal feudal relationships.
2 Spring and Autumn and Warring States period: As the power and independence of various states increased, the feudal tribute relationships gradually faded. However, on some diplomatic occasions, tributary acts still occurred as symbols of friendship and respect.
3 Qin and Han period: After the unification of the six states by Qin, China entered an era of centralization. The Han Dynasty further expanded its territory and established connections with farther countries and regions. At this time, the Tribute System began to extend outward, including interactions with countries and regions in Central Asia, South Asia, and Southeast Asia. The interactions with the Western Regions during Emperor Wu of Han's reign, such as the struggle with the Xiongnu and Zhang Qian's mission to the Western Regions, strengthened this system.

The Tribute System was further developed and refined in subsequent dynasties, such as Tang, Song, Yuan, Ming, and Qing. Especially during the Ming and Qing dynasties, the Tribute System was significantly evident with frequent interactions with countries in East Asia, South Asia, and Southeast Asia.

In summary, China's Tribute System initially was based on internal feudal relationships, but over time, it gradually expanded outward, establishing economic and diplomatic connections with more distant countries and regions.

The Tributary System was the institutional embodiment of ancient Chinese economic statecraft, likely representing the longest-standing institution of economic statecraft in history. The key dimensions of the Tributary System are as follows:

1 Economic Non-Reciprocity: Although peripheral countries or regimes offered tributes to the central empire, it wasn't one-sided. Chinese emperors often reciprocated with gifts far exceeding the received tributes. Thus, for many smaller countries, participating in the Tribute System was economically beneficial. However, for China, this system entailed significant financial burdens as the contributions required from the Central Kingdom far outweighed those received from the tributary states.
2 Trade and Economic Exchange: Official trade activities often accompanied the Tribute System. Tribute delegations often provided cover for

merchants who seized these opportunities for trade activities, thereby promoting economic exchanges between China and neighboring countries.

3 Economic Stability and Peace: The Tribute System enhanced economic connections and interdependence, promoting regional peace and stability to a certain extent. When economic interests are closely related, the risk of conflict may reduce.
4 Economic Influence: Through the Tribute System, China expanded its economic and cultural influence. Neighboring countries might adopt Chinese technologies, products, and culture, deepening economic ties with China.
5 Tool of Diplomatic Strategies: Dynasties in Chinese history utilized the Tribute System as part of their economic diplomatic strategies to ensure regional peace, stability, and influence.

In total, the Tribute System was a crucial part of ancient China's economic statecraft, promoting peace, cooperation, and mutually beneficial relationships with neighboring countries through economic means.

The Ming Dynasty (1368 AD–1644 AD) was one of the periods when the Chinese tributary system was most developed and active. During the Ming Dynasty, the tributary system, as a means of international relations and foreign policy, reached a relatively mature and systematic level. During the Ming Dynasty, due to its strong economic and military power, as well as the development of maritime trade and diplomacy, many countries and regions established tribute relationships with the Ming Dynasty. Some of the tributary countries or regions during this period include: (1) East Asia: Korea and Japan (though the tribute relationship with Ming was unstable and sometimes interrupted); (2) Southeast Asia: Vietnam, Siam (present-day Thailand), Malay states (including parts of present-day Malaysia and Indonesia), Brunei and Parts of the Philippines; (3) South Asia: Ceylon (present-day Sri Lanka); (4) Central and West Asia: Occasionally, envoys, merchants, or delegations from Central and West Asia would visit Ming, though this was slightly different from the fixed tribute relationships with East and Southeast Asia; and (5) Africa: Due to Admiral Zheng He's seven voyages to the Western Seas, connections were established with some countries and city-states along the eastern coast of Africa, such as Mogadishu, Muscat, and Malindi.

It should be noted that the tribute relationships did not imply that these countries were vassal states or territories of Ming. Instead, the Tribute System was more of a diplomatic and economic interaction method, through which trade, cultural exchanges, and political communications were conducted. Although at times conflicts and disputes existed, the Tribute System mainly served as a way for peripheral countries or regimes to offer tributes to central major countries (like China) to show loyalty and respect, expecting reciprocations, protection, or recognition in return. While in some cases, military aid or protection might be provided to tributary states by the central major country, the Tribute System didn't automatically imply such military obligations or commitments.

That being said, China did send troops to protect the tributary states and tried to maintain the Tributary System. Here are some obvious examples:

1 Wars with Vietnam:

   - Han-Nanyue War: From 111 BC to 108 BC, Emperor Wu of Han launched a conquest war against the Kingdom of Nanyue to unify the southern frontier. Although there was a tribute relationship between Nanyue and the Han Dynasty before this, military action was taken by the Han when Nanyue threatened Han's interests.
   - Ming-Annam War: During the Ming Dynasty, Ming forces militarily intervened in Annam (now northern Vietnam) multiple times. Especially during the reigns of Yongle and Xuande, the Ming Dynasty sent troops to Annam multiple times to support their own candidates for tributary states.

2 Wars with Mongolia: The relationship between the Ming Dynasty and Mongolia was sometimes good and sometimes bad, and both sides had periods of accepting each other's tributary relations. When the threat from Mongolia to Ming increased, the Ming Dynasty carried out military actions multiple times, such as the expeditions sent by Emperor Taizu to pacify Mongolia.
3 Wars with Japan: The Yuan Dynasty launched two famous Mongol invasions when trying to conquer Japan (1274 and 1281). Although there was a tributary relationship between Japan and the Yuan Dynasty before this, military action was taken by the Yuan Dynasty when Japan rejected the Yuan's demands.
4 Military Intervention in Ryukyu: The Ming Dynasty had sent troops in the early days to support the Ryukyu Kingdom, which had a tributary relationship with it, to help stabilize its regime.

To maintain the Tributary System was costly and often led to overextension. As a matter of fact, the high cost of maintaining the Tributary System was a key factor of the collapse of the Ming Dynasty and the Qing Dynasty, the last two dynasties in Chinese history. At the end of the 16th century, Japan's Toyotomi Hideyoshi planned to invade Korea as part of his continental expansion strategy, ultimately intending to attack the Ming Dynasty. In 1592, Japan invaded Korea, quickly occupying most regions. The Korean Dynasty requested assistance from the Ming Dynasty in this dire situation. The Ming Dynasty saw Japan's actions as a threat to its own security and felt responsible for assisting a long-term tributary state, deciding to send troops to aid Korea. This war lasted six years, until 1598, when Toyotomi Hideyoshi died, and Japan decided to withdraw its troops.[6]

The Imjin War (1592–1598) posed a significant burden on the treasury of the Ming Dynasty. To support this war, the Ming Dynasty mobilized a large amount of financial resources, materials, and manpower. According to historical records, the Ming Dynasty invested large amounts of food, gold and silver, weapons, and other materials in this war. This war not only consumed the economic resources of the Ming Dynasty but also resulted in a large number of soldiers being killed or injured. Additionally, to maintain frontline operations, the Ming Dynasty also needed to frequently levy taxes and conscript soldiers, leading to domestic dissatisfaction and difficulties. The pressure of this war on the Ming Dynasty's treasury was so great that sometimes emergency financial measures, such as issuing paper money, were necessary to raise funds.

The economic pressure brought by this war also affected the political stability of the Ming Dynasty. Although the Ming Dynasty successfully assisted Korea and won the war, long-term military expenditures emptied the treasury, and together with other domestic and foreign pressures, it laid the groundwork for the ultimate decline of the Ming Dynasty. Forty-six years later since the end of Imjin War, the Ming Dynasty finally collapsed in 1644 amid the peasant rebellion led by Li Zicheng. Li Zicheng was finally defeated by the Qing forces, who established China's last imperial dynasty, Qing Dynasty (1644 AD–1912 AD).

History repeats itself. The Qing Dynasty sent troops to Korea once again to maintain its Tribute System, with Japan emerging as the rival. China and Japan fought in the Battle of Jiawu (1894–1895), also known as the First Sino-Japanese War, or the Battle of the Yalu River. This battle further weakened the Qing Dynasty and brought tremendous humiliations to the Chinese nation. One of the direct consequences of this war was the signing of the Treaty of Shimonoseki, according to which China was forced to cede Taiwan and its affiliated islands to Japan.

In the late 19th century, although the Kingdom of Korea was nominally a tributary state of the Qing Dynasty, due to internal political and economic turmoil, a series of reformist and anti-reform factions emerged within the country. These factions often sought the support of external major powers, especially the Qing Dynasty and Japan, to consolidate or expand their power. Over time, Japan's influence on the Korean Peninsula gradually increased, conflicting with the influence of the Qing Dynasty.

In 1894, the Donghak Peasant Revolution occurred in Korea. The Korean government requested the Qing Dynasty to send troops to help suppress the uprising, and the Qing Dynasty complied and dispatched troops. However, Japan also took the opportunity to send troops to Korea, claiming it was to protect Japanese citizens and their interests in Korea, leading to a direct confrontation between Chinese and Japanese forces on the Korean Peninsula.

The tense situation between the two sides in Korea quickly escalated into a full-scale war. In the subsequent military conflicts, the Battle of the Yalu River was the most crucial naval battle, in which the Japanese navy achieved a decisive victory.

The two historical periods, the Ming Dynasty (1368–1644 AD) and the Qing Dynasty (1644–1912 AD), spanning more than 500 years, collectively demonstrate the significant importance of the Tribute System in China's history. Maintaining the Tribute System was crucial for upholding the legitimacy of the imperial dynasties in China. However, the cost of doing so often resulted in the overextension and subsequent collapse of these imperial dynasties. Therefore, economic statecraft in ancient China was much more than a mere tactic or craft; it was integral to the survival of the dynasty and the international order that underpinned these dynasties.

1.4 Historical Initiatives of China's Economic Statecraft

Economic statecraft refers to a country using economic means to achieve diplomatic or strategic objectives, or the other way around. In Chinese history, there were many initiatives of economic statecraft. Below are some examples:

1. Silk Road: Starting from the Han Dynasty (202 BC–9 AD, 25–220 AD), the Silk Road was a trade and cultural exchange route connecting China with Western Asia, South Asia, and even Europe. It was not just a commercial route but also a channel for political and cultural exchange. During the reign of Emperor Wu of Han, Zhang Qian was sent to the Western Regions, successfully opening this route, allowing goods like silk and tea from China to flow into the West, while also enabling cultural exchanges with foreign regions.
2. Maritime Silk Road: South of the Silk Road, the Maritime Silk Road became another essential trade and cultural exchange route connecting China, Southeast Asia, South Asia, and East Africa. During the Tang and Song Dynasties, maritime trade flourished, and port cities like Quanzhou and Guangzhou had close ties with foreign countries. In the early 15th century, Admiral Zheng He made seven voyages to regions such as Southeast Asia, South Asia, the Middle East, and even East Africa. Although these voyages were mainly to display the power of the Ming Dynasty, they also boosted trade and cultural exchanges with these regions.
3. Tea-Horse Trade with Central and Western Asia during the Ming and Qing Dynasties: During the Ming and Qing Dynasties, Chinese tea was transported to Tibet and then entered Central and Western Asia via the Himalayas. Meanwhile, horses and other goods from foreign regions also entered China. This tea-horse trade had economic significance as well as political and strategic meanings.
4. Maritime Prohibition Policies: The maritime prohibition policies in the middle and late Ming Dynasty and early Qing Dynasty restricted China's maritime trade with the outside world to protect the domestic economy and maintain national security. Before the Opium Wars in 1840s, the Qing Dynasty implemented a restricted foreign trade policy. This included

establishing "official merchant houses" for official trade and a single trading port system in Guangzhou. The maritime prohibition policies, representing a form of negative economic statecraft, were the opposite of the Silk Road policies, which exemplified positive economic statecraft.

A significant example of China's positive economic statecraft initiative was Admiral Zheng He's voyages. Zheng He's seven voyages took place between 1405 and 1433 AD and were major diplomatic activities during the reigns of Emperor Yongle and Emperor Xuande of the Ming Dynasty. The main purpose of Zheng He's voyages was to display the authority and wealth of the Ming Dynasty and to establish diplomatic relations and expand the influence of the Ming Dynasty. This was a "great power diplomacy" strategy, spreading the culture and influence of the Ming Dynasty through peaceful means.

During Zheng He's voyages, although the Ming government allowed and supported these voyages, there were still strict restrictions on private maritime trade. This led to a contradictory situation: the government-approved and supported Zheng He's voyages contrasted with the restrictive policies on private trade. After Zheng He's death, the Ming Dynasty gradually abandoned this large-scale maritime diplomatic strategy. Meanwhile, the sea ban policy was further strengthened after Emperor Xuande.

1.5 Major Challenges for China's Classic Economic Statecraft

China's economic statecraft has an inbuilt problem: overstretching. Maintaining a moral-based international order through the Tribute System was costly. In the Ming Dynasty, especially after Zheng He's voyages, opposition voices appeared advocating for saving fiscal expenditures, concentrating resources on inland defense, and holding skeptical or even opposing attitudes toward maritime activities. This led to the restriction of maritime activities and the neglect or destruction of related materials.

It is important to remember that the Tribute System was neither a form of free trade as advocated by liberalism, nor was it an export-oriented trade as championed by Mercantilism. The Tribute System was built upon state-led, non-reciprocal trade and the granting of gifts.

Zheng He's voyages caused a financial crisis: his voyages were primarily tribute missions, politically motivated, and overlooked practical economic benefits, often referred to as "generous outbound, meager return". Historical records show that the grand rewards by Zheng He and Emperor Zhu Di to these foreign tributaries triggered panic in the empire. Just the expense on silver alone was six million taels per year, not including rewards for the 20,000 officials and soldiers. Due to the large amount of copper coins carried abroad for purchases, there was a significant outflow of currency, causing a domestic "money shortage", severely depleting the national reserves and causing a massive devaluation of the currency.

Moreover, Zheng He's economic statecraft was state monopoly: on the surface, Zheng He's fleet, each time it set sail, was magnificent and awe-inspiring, "cloudy sails blocking the sun", but essentially, it was a "lonely sail in the distance". Behind it, there were no, nor were they allowed, ships from private maritime merchants. Emperor Zhu Di did not allow coastal military and civilians to "privately interact with foreign countries", repeatedly ordering "strict prohibition against civilians sailing overseas privately". As for the overseas trade of coastal residents, he ordered it to be "strictly prohibited and completely stopped". The strict maritime prohibition jeopardized the livelihoods of coastal residents and also led to the closure of the seas when the state-organized voyages of Zheng He stopped. In other words, once the royal needs were met, once they heard the news of peace and tranquility, the ocean was completely closed off from the national level to the civilian level, resulting in the absence of the ocean in China's modern history at a critical period in world history.

When discussing economic statecraft, people tend to forget the following three key contradictions:

- The contradiction between the relative scarcity of national wealth and the unlimited nature of a state's pursuit of power.
- The contradiction between the scarcity of state power and the unlimited pursuit of wealth by the state.
- Finally, there exists a dialectical relationship between a state's wealth strategy and power strategy, characterized by contradictions and complementarities, mutually shaping and constructing each other (Zhang, 2023, pp. 17–18).

Emperor Yang Guang of the Sui Dynasty was a typical example of wealth-power dialectic. He was the second and last emperor of China's Sui Dynasty, ruling from 604 to 618 AD. He is a highly controversial figure in history, marked by both his impressive achievements and the socioeconomic problems they engendered.

His major accomplishments included: (1) Completing the construction of the Sui Dynasty's capital, Daxing City (present-day Beijing); (2) Strengthening centralized power through a series of administrative reforms; and (3) Constructing the Grand Canal, connecting China's north and south, facilitating economic and cultural exchange.

However, his rule was also plagued with significant issues:

1 His investment in costly construction projects, such as Daxing City and the Grand Canal, exacerbated the state's financial burdens and the taxation pressure on the people.
2 He initiated three costly military campaigns against Goguryeo (located in present-day Korean Peninsula and Northeast China), all ending in failure and draining national resources.

3 In the later years of his rule, political corruption, embezzlement, and tyranny led to widespread public dissatisfaction, ultimately sparking rebellion.

In 618 AD, Emperor Yang was assassinated, leading to the collapse of the Sui Dynasty and ushering in a new era in Chinese history—the Tang Dynasty. Tang Dynasty literary scholar Pi Rixiu wrote "Two Odes to the Reminiscence of the Bian River" to praise the achievements of Emperor Yang Guang. The first one: "Thousands of dragon boats with green silk sails, all reaching Yangzhou, never to return. It must be heaven's instruction to open the Bian waterway, making a flat land for over a thousand miles without any mountains". The second one: "Everyone says the fall of the Sui was because of this river, yet today for a thousand miles, it still relies on its flowing waves. If it weren't for the dragon boat affairs at the water palace, in discussing achievements, it would be much more than those of Yu".[7]

In the second half of the 19th century, China's Tribute System began to collapse due to the internal weaknesses of the Qing Dynasty, Western imperialism and unequal treaties, Japanese aggression in East Asia, and the influence of nationalism and the concept of the modern nation-state. With the demise of the Tribute System came the end of China's classic economic statecraft. However, Confucianism, particularly the teachings of Confucius and Mencius, remains the most influential philosophy in China. The Tribute System remains a prominent historical example from which Chinese policymakers continue to draw lessons and inspiration.

The Tribute System of China, though historically concluded, still holds certain relevance for China's economic statecraft today. It was based on cultural and political exchanges, emphasizing the establishment of relationships and networks. This way of thinking still echoes in China's current foreign policy, such as in promoting the Belt and Road Initiative, where the focus is on cooperation and mutual benefit, not just economic interests.

The Tribute System was centered on managing asymmetrical economic relations. This experience with unequal economic relationships remains relevant to China's current economic and diplomatic dealings, particularly with developing countries. As an inherently hierarchical system, the Tribute System is no longer suitable for today's international relations, making it impossible for China to reinstate a new Tribute System. It is crucial for China to critically assess the old Tribute System and consider the type of international order its new economic statecraft could help establish.

In the subsequent chapters that discuss China's new economic statecraft, we can still identify some distinct traces of the Tribute System, deeply rooted in the teachings of Confucius and Mencius.

Notes

1 "The Great Learning" originally was one of the chapters in the "Book of Rites" and is one of the Confucian classics. Regarding the authorship of "The Great Learning," there are various traditional viewpoints. The most widespread belief is that it

was recorded and compiled by Confucius's disciples and their later followers, but the specific author or editor is uncertain. In later annotations and interpretations, especially within the Neo-Confucianism of the Song and Ming dynasties, Zhu Xi re-annotated "The Great Learning" and grouped it with "The Doctrine of the Mean," "The Analects," and "Mencius," collectively known as the "Four Books." These books became the primary textbooks for scholars studying Confucianism during the Ming and Qing dynasties.

2 The discussion in this paragraph is based on a conversation with OpenAI's ChatGPT, where ChatGPT provided information and analysis based on its training data. The conversation took place on November 19, 2023.

3 《孟子》,《尽心章句上》"The 'Exhaustive Discussions' section in the 'Mencius' text."

Mencius, also known by his birth name Meng Ke or Mengzi, was a famous Chinese philosopher who lived during the Warring States period from around 372 to 289 BCE. He is best known as the most famous follower of Confucius and a significant contributor to Confucian philosophy. Mencius expanded and developed Confucius's ideas, emphasizing the inherent goodness of human nature (renxing) and the importance of nurturing one's moral qualities and virtues to realize one's full ethical potential. Mencius traveled from state to state, engaging with rulers and offering advice on governance and leadership based on Confucian principles. He believed that a ruler should be benevolent and virtuous to govern effectively and that the people's well-being should be a priority. Mencius argued that if a ruler failed to provide for the people and act virtuously, the people had the moral right to overthrow him.

His teachings and dialogues were later compiled into a text known as the "Mencius" or "Mengzi," which, along with the "Analects" of Confucius, became a central text in Confucian education. Along with Confucius and Xunzi, Mencius is considered one of the three most important Confucian philosophers, and his interpretations of Confucianism have been highly influential in the development of East Asian intellectual thought and moral philosophy.

Source: Content derived from a conversation with OpenAI's ChatGPT, accessed on November 19, 2023.

4 "The noble person is aware of morality, the lesser person is aware of profit." This statement is from the "Analects of Confucius - Yong Ye" chapter. This implies that noble individuals should be guided by morality, while lesser individuals are guided by profit.

5 Chinese Text Project, "梁惠王上-Liang Hui Wang I", available at: https://ctext.org/mengzi/liang-hui-wang-i

6 The emperor of the Ming Dynasty during the Imjin War (1592–1598) was Emperor Wanli. His name was Zhu Yijun, and he was the 13th emperor of the Ming Dynasty, ruling from 1572 to 1620, making him the longest-reigning emperor in the history of the Ming Dynasty. Under his rule, the Ming Dynasty experienced early prosperity, but subsequently also encountered various internal and external difficulties, including the Imjin War with Japan.

7 Yu refers to Yu the Great, a legendary ruler in ancient China famed for his introduction of flood control.

Reference List

Angus, M. (2007) *Development Centre Studies Chinese Economic Performance in the Long Run, 960–2030 AD, Second Edition, Revised and Updated.* Paris: OECD Publishing.

Zhang, X. T. (2023) *New Economic Statecraft: China, the United States and the European Union.* Oxford: Taylor & Francis.

2 China's Contemporary Economic Statecraft

A Marxist-Developmentalist Synthesis

Since the founding of the People's Republic of China (PRC) in 1949, the Communist Party of China (CPC) has maintained its hold on power, guiding the nation's economic statecraft with Marxist ideology. However, a closer examination reveals that the situation is not as clear-cut as it might initially appear. What we find about the guiding thoughts of China's economic statecraft post-1949 is a Marxist-Developmentalist synthesis.

Economic statecraft, by definition, involves the production of wealth and its conversion into power. Marxism, on the other hand, aims to achieve social justice through the redistribution of wealth. Thus, when a Marxist party governs a state and engages in statecraft, it faces an inherent dilemma between wealth creation and wealth distribution. In other words, a Marxist state must resolve this dilemma; failure to do so could lead to the downfall of the ruling Marxist party. Ultimately, wealth distribution is unsustainable without wealth creation.

For the first decade of Mao Zedong' s ruling, he understood very well that China was in a situation of "extremely poor and blank" ("一穷二白"). So, he and his comrades focused on industrialization, agriculture, and improving people's livelihoods. But he was too hasty in achieving Communism in China. His rash actions, including the "Three-Anti and Five-Anti Campaigns" ("三反五反"), "Great Leap Forward", ("大跃进") "Mass Steel Production" ("大炼钢铁"), and the goal to "Surpass the UK and Catch Up with the US" ("赶英超美"), led to catastrophe. Until Deng Xiaoping's time, Mao's wrongdoing has been corrected. Deng, as a Marxist, has adopted a pragmatic approach, which is a developmentalist approach.

This Marxist-Developmentalist synthesis is central to understanding the long-term rule of China's CPC. This synthesis alleviates the tensions inherent in Marxism, specifically the dilemma between wealth creation and wealth redistribution, or, in simpler terms, between economic efficiency and social justice. For any Marxist party to govern long-term, the key lies in striking a balance between efficiency and justice. The demise of the USSR was largely due to its failure to maintain this balance. Mao's mistakes were also related to this issue.

DOI: 10.4324/9781003270379-3

China's developmentalism is a combination of economic liberalism and mercantilism with a strong state. Since the People's Republic was founded in 1949, Chinese leaders have embraced different guiding thoughts of economic statecraft, ranging from Marxism and mercantilism to economic liberalism (Table 2.1).

In this chapter, we will discuss Mao Zedong's Marxist economic statecraft, Deng Xiaoping's developmentalist economic statecraft, and the continuation of Deng's approach by Jiang Zemin and Hu Jintao.

Table 2.1 China's Economic Statecraft from Mao Zedong to Xi Jinping

	Political ideology	*Economic ideology*	*Main tasks*	*Economic statecraft (Wealth-power strategy)*
Mao Zedong	Communist	Marxist mixed with China's traditional way of thinking as a central kingdom	Anti-imperialism, independence, self-sufficiency, building a strong state	Supporting Communist revolution, developing countries, supporting a new international economic order
Deng Xiaoping	Communist	Developmentalism (leaning toward liberalism)	Economic development, building a strong state	GATT accession
Jiang Zemin	Communist	Developmentalism (leaning toward liberalism)	Economic development, building a strong state, the great rejuvenation of China, "Three Represents"	GATT/WTO accession
Hu Jintao	Communist	Developmentalism (Liberalism + light Mercantilism + Socialism)	Economic development, building a strong state, great national rejuvenation The Outlook of Scientific Development	Emerging strategic industries, self-innovation

(Continued)

Table 2.1 (Continued)

	Political ideology	*Economic ideology*	*Main tasks*	*Economic statecraft (Wealth-power strategy)*
Xi Jinping	Communist	Developmentalism (Light/ controlled mercantilism + Liberalism + Socialism + Historic logic)	Building a strong state, the great rejuvenation of China Two "One-hundred Years", "China Dream"	BRI, AIIB, BRICS Development Bank; competitive regionalism, RCEP, FTAAP Free Trade Zone, Three Global Initiatives (Security, Development, and Civilization)

Source: Made by the author.

2.1 Marxist Economic Statecraft: Mao Zedong's Way

Mao Zedong is perceived in China as a savior of the Chinese people, defeating imperialism, feudalism, and bureaucratic capitalism. However, he also made significant mistakes, such as launching the Cultural Revolution.

The reason why Mao Zedong was idolized after 1949 is largely related to China's century of humiliation, starting with the Opium Wars in the 1840s. For nearly 100 years following these wars, various political parties and forces tried to save China, including Dr. Sun Yat-Sen and his Nationalist Party. Chiang Kai-shek fought against the Japanese invasion but failed to win the hearts and minds of the majority of Chinese people. The CPC succeeded in doing so, led by Mao Zedong.

In 1949, China was a very poor country, a country Chinese themselves called "utterly destitute" or "extremely poor and blank" ("一穷二白"). In terms of industrial structure, the new China established in 1949 was still an agricultural country. Only 12.6% of China's national income came from industry, while 68.4% came from agriculture (National Bureau of Statistics, 1979).

Therefore, when Mao began his rule over China, the most pressing challenges he faced were industrializing the nation and ensuring the survival of the new Communist regime amid the emerging tensions of the Cold War.

Mao Zedong's economic statecraft was a Marxist one. His priority was to eliminate capitalism and defeat imperialism. As Mao Zedong said at the Sixth Plenary Session of the Seventh Central Committee of the CPC in 1955,

"Marxism is quite fierce, there isn't much conscience, it aims to eradicate imperialism, feudalism, capitalism, and also small-scale production. In this aspect, having less conscience is better" (Mao, 1977).

Mao Zedong recognized the need for China to undergo a prolonged period of recuperation and rebuilding. However, he opted for a hastier approach, implementing a wartime economic statecraft rooted in his Marxist ideology.

During the "First Five-Year Plan" (1953–1957), the Chinese government implemented extensive nationalization and collectivization policies. These policies were focused primarily on the collectivization of agriculture and the socialist transformation of private industry and commerce. By 1960, China's private economy was essentially integrated into the state and collective framework, achieving the goals of socialist transformation.

The seven-year process of eliminating private economy (1953–1960) went through five stages: "sandwichization", "Five-Antis Tax Inspection", "marginalization", "fixed interest redemption", and "extinction" (Wu, 2013). By October 1952, with the end of the "Five-Antis Campaign", the examined and supplemented "five-poison accounts" reached over 300 billion yuan, which was more than half of the military expenses for Korea (Wu, 2013).

Around the time when the "First Five-Year Plan" ended in 1957, the Communists almost simultaneously achieved two significant victories: high-speed economic growth and the elimination of the private sector. This led to an unprecedented swelling of confidence among the decision-makers. Subsequently, they went further down the path of self-pride (Wu, 2013).

The "Great Leap Forward" starting in 1958 and the "Third Front" construction caused severe depletion of national strength. Mao's economic statecraft started to go wrong.

The goal of the "Great Leap Forward" in industry was to surpass the UK, while in agriculture, the aim was to double the output of grains and cotton within a year. Mao Zedong determined that the only metric for evaluating China's economic surpassing of the UK was steel production; thus, a nationwide steel smelting campaign was launched. There are indications in written communications from Mao to fellow party leaders in late 1958, that he intended the "Great Leap Forward" to be a "bridge" between socialism and communism (Bottelier, 2018). During the three years of natural disasters (1958–1962), Liu Shaoqi, the then Chinese President in charge of the economy, had to admit that the Great Famine was "three parts natural disaster, seven parts man-made calamity", suggesting that the "Great Leap Forward" had exacerbated the situation.

In the 1960s, the relationship between China and the Soviet Union, described as "teacher and brother", deteriorated significantly. The Soviet Union stationed a million troops on the Sino-Soviet and Sino-Mongolian borders. At the same time, the United States deployed troops to Vietnam, and China faced threats from two superpowers from both the south and north. The judgment within the Chinese Communist Party's decision-making circle was that "war was inevitable, and preparations should be made for a large-scale, early, and nuclear warfare". Based on this, the Chinese Communist Party Central Committee made a significant strategic decision for "Third Front Construction", relocating key industrial enterprises from the northeastern, northern, and eastern coastal regions to the western and northwestern regions.

To further understand Mao's Marxist and wartime economic statecraft, we need to solve three puzzles:

Puzzle One: How did China manage to achieve a stalemate with the United States during the Korean War?

China's involvement in the Korean War (1950–1953), dubbed as the "War to Resist America and Aid Korea" (抗美援朝), came at a time when the newly established PRC was economically fragile. The PRC was founded in 1949, just a year before the outbreak of the Korean War. China's GDP in 1952 accounted for 5.2% of the world's total, whereas the United States accounted for 27.5% (Angus, 2007). Indeed, it remains a mystery how China could fight the Korean War with such a thin economic foundation.

There are a few explanations about how China managed to finance its military involvement in the Korean War despite its economic challenges.

First, the Soviet Support. The Soviet Union was a significant ally to China during this period. Soviet military support, both in terms of equipment and advisory, was crucial for China. Soviet Premier Joseph Stalin provided substantial military assistance, including arms supplies and logistical support, which alleviated some financial pressure on China. That being said, the USSR did not send the ground troops during the Korean War. Therefore, for many Chinese, it was the Chinese People's Volunteer Army who almost single-handedly helped the Korean people to defend the outpost of socialism, which was invaluable for the defense security of the Soviet Union (Xie, 2002). The aid from the Soviet Union to China through 156 projects was implemented only after the end of the Korean War.

Second, the domestic mobilization and austerity measures. The Chinese government under Chairman Mao Zedong implemented austerity measures to mobilize domestic resources. This involved reducing expenditures in other areas and reallocating resources to the war effort. Under Mao's leadership, Chen Yun, who was in charge of financial and economic work, played a key role in wartime economics. Chen Yun's approach was to prepare for the worst while striving for the best outcomes, preferring to see the situation as worse so as to be prepared and remain unflustered when faced with issues, hence adhering to bottom-line thinking.

On October 26, 1950, Chen Yun submitted a written report to Mao Zedong and the Central Committee, making three estimates regarding the developments of the Korean War. The first scenario was border war with domestic peace; the second was border war with domestic bombings;

the third was border war with enemy landing at China's coast, plunging the entire nation into war. Chen Yun pointed out that the financial policy should be "based on war", and temporarily, the second scenario should be taken as the benchmark. At the same time, he proposed reducing economic investments and appropriately widening the price scissors between industrial and agricultural products to increase trade income, in order to cope with military expenditures and possible tax reductions post-bombings. On November 15, 1950, Chen Yun, during the national financial work conference, proposed the guideline of "national defense first, market stability second, others third", clarifying that all financial work should be subordinated to the war. Chen Yun also introduced the approach of "carving the radish" for expenditures and "milking the cow" for income; "carving the radish" meant reducing all possible expenditures, while "milking the cow" meant striving to increase any possible financial income, to fundamentally alleviate financial strain and meet the requirements of "national defense first" (Study Times, 2020).

Finally, revenue from state-owned enterprises. By 1950, many of the key industries in China were nationalized, and the revenue generated from these state-owned enterprises contributed to war financing.

Moreover, China utilized its foreign exchange reserves and gold holdings to finance military expenditures. The government issued war bonds and levied additional taxes to raise funds. The revenue collected from these sources was directed toward covering military expenses. These combined efforts and sources of financing enabled China to sustain its military involvement in the Korean War, despite its economically challenged situation.

Puzzle Two: What were the sources of revenue that sustained the economic statecraft during Mao's leadership?

Land reform is key. Mao once said, "Our liberation war (1945–1949) was mainly won by these 160 million people. With the victory of land reform, the victory over Chiang Kai-shek was achieved" (Mao, 2002). Overthrowing the landlord class and giving land to the peasants was Mao Zedong's economic governance technique. Land reform was both a profound economic transformation and a profound social and political transformation. Its completion not only mobilized the enthusiasm of the peasants but also maximized the cohesion and appeal of the Chinese Communist Party at the rural grassroots level, playing an important role in the establishment and consolidation of rural grassroots people's political power (Editorial Team of the Economic History of China, 2019).

The land reform in China, initiated after the establishment of the PRC in 1949, continued until 1953. This period marked the phase of nationwide land reform implementation by the Chinese Communist Party, aimed at abolishing the feudal landlord system and redistributing land to the peasants. By 1953, land reform was essentially completed in most regions, and China began transitioning to a collectivized model of agricultural production, known as the People's Commune movement. This movement signified a major shift in China's agricultural policies, from individual peasant farming to collective farming. Therefore, 1953 can be regarded as the end of the land reform period, after which Chinese agricultural and rural policies entered a new phase.

In parallel with land reform, China began to adopt the "New Democratic Economy". According to the Chinese official history book, the "New Democratic Economy" was a very beneficial attempt and a valuable exploration of China's developmental path made by the Chinese Communist Party (Editorial Team of the Economic History of China). The so-called "New Democratic Economy" refers to a transitional economy developing with the coexistence of various economic components under the leadership of the socialist nature of the state-owned economy; it is a socioeconomic form situated between capitalist economy and socialist economy (Editorial Team of the Economic History of China, 2019).

In summary, Mao Zedong's early rule over China did recognize the need for China to undergo a period of recuperation and rebuilding. However, since the late 1950s, he opted for a hastier approach, implementing "Great Leap Forward", "Mass Steel Production", and the goal to "Surpass the UK and Catch Up with the US", which finally led to economic and political catastrophe.

Puzzle Three: What is the relationship between Mao Zedong's Communist beliefs and the mistakes he made in economic statecraft?

First, the mismatch between ideals and reality. Mao's Communist beliefs emphasized idealized social and economic goals, such as class struggle, agricultural collectivization, and rapid industrial development. These ideals sometimes conflicted with China's economic realities and technical capabilities, leading to policy mistakes.

Second, overly rapid policies. Mao often adopted a radical approach in driving economic development and transformation, exemplified by the "Great Leap Forward" campaign. This policy aimed to achieve massive leaps in industry and agriculture in a short time but led to severe economic consequences, such as famine and resource wastage, due to a lack of practical considerations.

From the analysis of the three aforementioned puzzles, it becomes evident that Mao's economic statecraft was fundamentally Marxist and shaped by wartime conditions. It seems that Mao never walked out of his wartime political economy. While it was effective in addressing war-related challenges, it proved unsustainable. Mao's staunch Communist beliefs played a crucial role in protecting the nascent Communist regime and enabled the new China to resist imperialism and feudalism. However, these beliefs often led to the neglect of economic realities and expertise, resulting in a series of economic missteps and challenges.

2.2 Developmentalist Economic Statecraft: Deng Xiaoping's Way

When Mao Zedong passed away on September 9, 1976, China's economy was teetering on the brink of collapse. Although Mao's death marked a turning point, the formal end of the Cultural Revolution was announced by his successor, Chairman Hua Guofeng, in October 1976. Shortly thereafter, Deng Xiaoping emerged as the core leader among Chinese political elites. He believed that China urgently needed a pivotal change to avert further crisis.

Deng Xiaoping's perspectives on both internal and global contexts significantly differed from those of Mao Zedong. Deng believed that a third world war was not imminent, emphasizing instead that the major challenges faced were related to economic development. In comparison to the Communist beliefs held by Mao, Deng was less idealistic and more pragmatic. Furthermore, there were notable differences in economic statecraft between Mao Zedong and Deng Xiaoping.

Deng Xiaoping believed that "Development is the absolute principle", "Seek truth from facts", "Practice is the sole criterion for testing truth" and "Let some people get rich first".

Although both Mao Zedong and Deng Xiaoping firmly believed in Communism and emphasized the central leadership role of the CPC, Deng's approach to economic statecraft aligned more with developmentalism rather than adhering to the Lenin-Stalin model of Marxist economic policies. Here, developmentalism refers to a set of economic policies and practices focused primarily on fostering the growth and development of a nation's economy.[1]

The key differences between Mao Zedong and Deng Xiaoping in economic statecraft are as follows:

> Firstly, on economic development strategy. Mao Zedong valued politics and ideology more, and tended to achieve economic and social goals through large-scale social movements, such as the "Great Leap Forward". Deng Xiaoping emphasized that "development is the absolute principle", proposed the "reform and opening up" strategy, and advocated market economic reforms while maintaining the leadership of the Party.
>
> Secondly, on ideology and practice. Mao Zedong emphasized revolution and struggle, often launching movements to transform society and people's thoughts. Deng Xiaoping proposed the idea of "seeking truth from facts", believing that policies and strategies should be adjusted according to actual conditions. Deng Xiaoping addressed the Chinese people's worship of Mao and aimed to end the lingering effects of the Cultural Revolution after 1976 by initiating a significant debate on "the criterion of truth".
>
> On February 7, 1977, the "Two Newspapers and One Magazine"[2] published an editorial titled "Learn the Documents Well and Grasp the Main Issues," which stated, "We resolutely uphold *whatever* decision made by

Chairman Mao, and we always unswervingly follow *whatever* directive of Chairman Mao." The public introduction of the "Two Whatevers" sparked a major discussion throughout the Party regarding the criterion of truth. On May 11, the "Guangming Daily" published a special commentator's article titled "Practice is the Sole Criterion for Testing Truth." The publication of this article immediately sparked heated discussions and had a tremendous impact. This debate over the criterion of truth was not just an ordinary philosophical argument, but a fundamental rectification of chaos in terms of thought and theory. Deng Xiaoping encouraged and led this debate about the "criterion of truth" and liberated the entire party and people of the nation from the mental shackles of dogmatism and personality cult. This debate also helped reestablish the party's ideological line of seeking truth from facts, starting from reality in everything, and integrating theory with practice, thus preparing the ideological groundwork for further rectification of chaos (News of the Communist Party of China, 2023). This debate paved the way for reform and opening-up.

Thirdly, on foreign relations. During Mao Zedong's time, despite tensions with the Soviet Union at certain periods, there was still a tendency to unite with socialist countries. During Deng Xiaoping's time, China paid more attention to economic and diplomatic relations with all countries, including Western countries, and foreign strategies were no longer purely based on ideology. In other words, Mao's economic statecraft, rooted in Marxist ideology, was practiced along the geopolitical divide of East vs. West. In contrast, Deng Xiaoping's economic statecraft, prioritizing China's needs for economic development, extended globally, transcending ideological boundaries.

Fourthly, on the attitude towards economic reform. Mao Zedong was vigilant against capitalist tendencies and the danger of "taking the capitalist road". Deng Xiaoping believed that some "capitalist" phenomena must be tolerated in the reform, and proposed the view of "letting some people get rich first". Different from Mao Zedong, Deng Xiaoping believed that engaging in theoretical debates would lead to missed opportunities and lost chances for development. Fruitless arguments are of no help; truth can only be tested in practice. We should boldly experiment and try things out, refraining from drawing conclusions prematurely; action should speak for itself. "It doesn't matter if a cat is black or white; as long as it catches mice, it's a good cat." (China News, 2008) During the Cultural Revolution, the metaphor of "yellow cats and black cats" was criticized as "only caring about productivity" and faced condemnation. Around 1976, Mao Zedong specifically criticized Deng Xiaoping. Mao said, "This person"—referring to Deng Xiaoping—"does not focus on class struggle; he has never emphasized this key issue. It's still about the 'white cat, black cat,' regardless of whether it's imperialism or Marxism."

(China News, 2008)

In summary, Mao Zedong's Communist beliefs were more focused on ideology and politics, while Deng Xiaoping paid more attention to pragmatism and economic development. If we describe Mao's economic statecraft as staunchly Marxist, then Deng's economic statecraft should be characterized as pragmatically developmentalist.

When practicing economic statecraft, Deng Xiaoping very much emphasized enhancement and development of China's national economic strength. Here are some of Deng Xiaoping's core understandings and policy views on China's national economic strength:

> Firstly, supremacy of economic construction. Deng Xiaoping emphasized the importance of China's national economic construction. He believed that China's economic strength is the foundation for achieving national prosperity and modernization. He proposed the view that "development is the absolute principle", emphasizing that economic growth is China's most urgent task.
>
> Secondly, Reform and Opening Up Policy. Deng Xiaoping led China's reform and opening up policy, one of the core objectives of this policy is to improve China's economic strength through market-oriented reforms and opening up to the outside world. He introduced a series of reform measures, including the rural land contract system, state-owned enterprise reforms, and foreign investment, to promote rapid economic growth and modernization.
>
> Thirdly, "Socialism with Chinese Characteristics". Deng Xiaoping proposed the concept of "socialism with Chinese characteristics", emphasizing that China can develop its unique economic path within the framework of socialism. He believed that China could maintain political stability and the socialist system while absorbing international experience and market mechanisms to enhance the country's economic strength.
>
> Fourthly, emphasis on infrastructure construction. Deng Xiaoping believed that infrastructure construction is a key component of national economic strength. He supported investment in transportation, energy, communications, and other infrastructure sectors to support China's modernization construction and economic growth.
>
> Fifthly, international cooperation and opening-up. Deng Xiaoping advocated actively participating in international economic cooperation, absorbing external resources and technology to promote China's modernization. He encouraged foreign investment and technology introduction, while also advocating the "Five Principles of Peaceful Coexistence" to maintain international peace and stability.

In general, Deng Xiaoping's core views on China's national economic strength include the supremacy of economic construction, reform and opening up, socialism with Chinese characteristics, infrastructure construction, and international cooperation. Under his leadership, China achieved significant economic development, realizing the goals of national prosperity and modernization. These understandings and policy views became the cornerstone of China's reform, opening up, and economic development.

However, we need to understand Deng Xiaoping's economic statecraft was far from a capitalist one. There was a clear political boundary, which is China's Communist regime. That is why Deng emphasized the "Four Cardinal Principles", also known as the "Four Upholds": (1) Upholding the socialist path; (2) Upholding the dictatorship of the proletariat; (3) Upholding the leadership of the Communist Party; and (4) Upholding Marxism-Leninism and Mao Zedong Thought. Deng Xiaoping's economic liberalism, operating under the umbrella of Communism, significantly shaped China's economic statecraft in the ensuing decades.

These principles hold a significant position in China's political life and are considered the foundation of the theory and practice of socialism with Chinese characteristics. Despite adjustments and flexibility in actual policies and economic reforms, these Four Cardinal Principles are still regarded as unshakable guidelines.

After a decade of recovery growth, China's economy began to experience cyclical fluctuations. With the rapid development of light industries, the number of private enterprises surged, material supplies became increasingly tight, and nationwide prices started to soar uncontrollably. Illegal reselling of materials became rampant, and the reform of the contracting system in state-owned enterprises never fully materialized, resulting in substantial financial losses and heavier fiscal burdens. To break free from this predicament, the central government was forced to increase currency issuance, further accelerating inflation. Amidst these crises, decision-makers accepted opinions like those of Wu Jinglian, deciding to take the risk of quickly adjusting prices to be regulated by the market. The failure of this price adjustment in 1988 was one of the most disheartening events in the economic reform history of New China and significantly altered China's path to modernization. This failure caused many reform initiatives that were already on the agenda at that time to be postponed, with some even being indefinitely delayed. In a certain sense, the failure to "break through" meant that China missed an opportunity to join the global wave of democratization (Wu, 2013).

2.3 A Continuation of Deng Xiaoping's Way: Economic Statecraft of Jiang Zemin (1989–2002)

Mao and Deng represent two different ways of China's modern economic statecraft. Mao is largely Marxist, while Deng is much more pragmatic and developmentalist. Both ways feed into their successor leaderships: Jiang Zemin, Hu Jintao, and Xi Jinping.

Following Deng Xiaoping's retirement, General Secretary and President Jiang Zemin held the reigns of the Chinese government. Jiang adhered to the line of reform and opening to the outside world designed by Deng. In the era of Jiang Zemin, China scored great achievements in economic diplomacy, opening up overseas markets, stabilizing resource supply, and improving the country's economic cooperation with foreign countries.

Jiang Zemin's era witnessed many significant historical incidents, such as "the June 4th Incident", the 1997 Southeast Asian Financial Crisis, 1999 NATO bombing of the Chinese Embassy in Yugoslavia, the collision of a US aircraft and a Chinese aircraft over the South China Sea in 2000, and the 9/11 attacks. But President Jiang Zemin strongly believed that despite all these challenges, the first 20 years of the 21st century was a period of strategic opportunities for China. It happened that he was right.

The overarching philosophy of Jiang Zemin's statecraft can be encapsulated in his "Three Represents" thought. Jiang Zemin's "Three Represents" thought was proposed in the year 2000. Specifically, he first put forward the "Three Represents" thought on February 25, 2000, when he explicitly stated during his inspection work in Guangdong Province that the CPC must always represent the development requirements of China's advanced productive forces, always represent the forward direction of China's advanced culture, and always represent the fundamental interests of the broadest masses of the Chinese people (Li, 2022). This thought later became one of the guiding ideologies of the CPC.

Jiang Zemin said: "The thought of the 'Three Represents' did not emerge out of thin air. It is the result of our continuous exploration and development in theory and practice over the past thirteen years"… Especially at the end of the 1980s and the beginning of the 1990s, when serious political turmoil occurred domestically, dramatic changes in Eastern Europe, the disintegration of the Soviet Union, and serious setbacks in world socialism, China's socialist cause faced unprecedented difficulties and pressures. Our Party and country were at a crucial historical juncture that would determine their future and destiny (Hu, 2016).

Guided by his belief in the "strategic opportunity period" and the "Three Represents" thought, Jiang continued to implement economic statecraft in the manner established by Deng Xiaoping. Jiang Zemin's economic statecraft primarily revolved around the continuation and expansion of the economic reforms that had been initiated by his predecessors, Deng Xiaoping and Hu Yaobang. Jiang's economic strategies were characterized by several key elements:

> Firstly, Market-Oriented Reforms. Jiang promoted market-oriented reforms, including the restructuring of state-owned enterprises (SOEs) to improve efficiency and competitiveness. He also encouraged the development of the private sector and foreign direct investment.

Secondly, "Three Represents". Jiang's "Three Represents" theory emphasized that the Communist Party should represent the development trend of China's advanced productive forces, the orientation of China's advanced culture, and the fundamental interests of the overwhelming majority of the Chinese people. This also had economic implications, emphasizing the role of entrepreneurs and technological advancements in China's development. During Jiang Zemin's era, capitalists could also join the Party. This refers to the significant policy shift made by the Communist Party of China (CPC) under Jiang Zemin's leadership to allow private entrepreneurs (capitalists) to become Party members. This change in policy reflected the Party's adaptation to the evolving economic structure of China, especially against the backdrop of the advancing reform and opening-up policies.

In traditional communist theory, capitalists were considered a class antagonistic to socialism. However, under Jiang's leadership, the CPC gradually recognized that with the development of the market economy, private entrepreneurs had become an important force in China's economic growth. Therefore, to better facilitate national economic development, the Party began to admit private entrepreneurs as its members.

Thirdly, "Going Out" Strategy. Jiang promoted the "Going Out" strategy, encouraging Chinese enterprises to invest overseas, seek international cooperation, and explore global markets.

Fourthly, engagement with global economy. Jiang encouraged China's participation in global economic institutions and frameworks, paving the way for China's accession to the World Trade Organization (WTO) in 2001. His leadership was crucial in negotiating and facilitating China's integration into the global economic system.

Fifthly, development of Western China. Jiang initiated strategies like the "Go West" policy, aimed at reducing regional disparities by promoting economic development in western and central provinces.

Sixthly, promotion of a Socialist Market Economy. Jiang worked on defining and promoting the concept of a "socialist market economy," blending elements of socialism with market economy principles. Jiang saw this as one of his biggest achievements in statecraft.

Jiang Zemin's economic statecraft was about strategically employing economic resources and policies to facilitate China's comprehensive development, global economic integration, and enhancing China's influence and competitiveness on the world stage. His leadership was instrumental in shaping China's economic trajectory in the global landscape and laying the foundations for its subsequent rapid economic rise.

However, Jiang Zemin's economic statecraft faced several major challenges during his tenure as China's leader. Some of the most significant challenges included:

Firstly, State-Owned Enterprises (SOEs) Reform. Reforming SOEs to improve efficiency and competitiveness while managing unemployment and social instability that might arise due to layoffs and restructuring was a major challenge.

Secondly, Regional Disparities. Addressing regional disparities in economic development, especially between the more developed coastal regions and the less developed western and central regions, was a persistent issue.

Thirdly, financial sector vulnerabilities. The Chinese banking and financial sectors faced issues like non-performing loans and required substantial reforms to improve their resilience and modernization.

Fourthly, legal and regulatory frameworks. Building robust legal and regulatory frameworks to support a market-oriented economy, protect property rights, and facilitate foreign investment and business operations was essential.

Fifthly, managing economic growth with social stability. Ensuring that economic reforms and growth did not lead to excessive social inequality or instability was crucial. Managing the social impacts of rapid economic changes, such as unemployment and labor mobility, required careful consideration.

Sixthly, global economic integration. Navigating China's accession to the World Trade Organization (WTO) and managing the implications of deeper global economic integration, such as increased competition and exposure to global market fluctuations, were significant challenges.

Seventhly, environmental sustainability. Managing the environmental impacts of rapid industrialization and economic growth, and promoting sustainable development practices was a growing concern.

Eighthly, innovation and technology. Promoting technological innovation and upgrading industries to move up the global value chain and reduce dependency on low-value-added manufacturing was a strategic challenge.

Ninthly, corruption and governance. Combating corruption and improving governance and bureaucratic efficiencies within the party and government apparatus were also continuous challenges.

Each of these challenges required strategic policy responses and governance adaptations. Jiang's economic statecraft was characterized by navigating through these complexities to maintain a trajectory of rapid economic development and reform while ensuring social stability and resilience against global economic uncertainties.

After the 1990s, a subtle shift in China's economic policy objectives occurred: the goal for the previous decade was economic recovery and solving the problem of insufficient production capacity, thus indulging the private sector. Everything beneficial to improving productivity was encouraged, even if it crossed legal boundaries, it was tolerated. After this period, the objective changed, shifting toward strengthening the leadership ability of the ruling group, enhancing control, and obtaining greater benefits in development. Consequently, the central government reclaimed powers from local authorities, and the government competed with the private sector for benefits, marking a return to authoritarianism (Wu, 2013). Starting in 1994, the implementation of a tax-sharing system had a significant impact on China's economic landscape thereafter. In 1994, the central government's fiscal revenue surged by 200% compared to the previous year. The most important outcome of this was that the central government regained the initiative in economic power and benefit distribution (Wu, 2013).

Gradually, Jiang's economic statecraft is assuming an increasingly salient developmentalist characteristic, with the central government playing a bigger role. There is a clear shift toward state intervention.

2.4 A Continuation of Deng Xiaoping's Way: Economic Statecraft of Hu Jintao (2002–2012)

Inherited from Deng Xiaoping and Jiang Zemin, Hu Jintao continued China's developmentalist economic statecraft. Hu's economic statecraft is theorized as the "Scientific Development" philosophy.

The outbreak of Severe Acute Respiratory Syndrome (SARS)[3] in 2003 was closely related to the proposal of the "Scientific Development" Concept. The Scientific Development Concept, proposed in 2003, was the first major challenge faced by Hu Jintao after taking office and had a significant impact on the formation of his thoughts on scientific development.

The outbreak and spread of SARS exposed new contradictions and problems in China after a phase of rapid economic development, such as uncoordinated development, lagging public health development, and an inadequate emergency response mechanism. This prompted the CPC Central Committee to deeply ponder over the development issues of China under the new situation. The major theoretical and practical question of "what kind of development to achieve and how to develop" was historically placed before the Chinese Communists.

At the end of August and the beginning of September 2003, during his inspection in Jiangxi, Hu Jintao proposed the concept of the Scientific

Development Concept, emphasizing the need to firmly establish a scientific view of coordinated, comprehensive, and sustainable development. In October, the Third Plenary Session of the 16th CPC Central Committee first formally put forward the Scientific Development Concept in the Party's official document, stressing "adherence to people-oriented principles, establishing a comprehensive, coordinated, and sustainable view of development, and promoting the comprehensive development of the economy, society, and people".

On March 10, 2004, Hu Jintao made a comprehensive explanation of the scientific connotation, basic requirements, and guiding significance of the Scientific Development Concept at the Central Population Resources and Environment Work Symposium. He pointed out that *adhering to people-oriented principles* means aiming for the comprehensive development of people, seeking and promoting development based on the fundamental interests of the people, continuously meeting the growing material and cultural needs of the people, effectively safeguarding the economic, political, and cultural rights and interests of the people, and allowing the fruits of development to benefit all the people. *Comprehensive development* means centering on economic construction, comprehensively advancing the construction of the economy, politics, and culture, and achieving economic development and overall social progress. *Coordinated development* means coordinating urban and rural development, regional development, economic and social development, harmonious development between man and nature, coordinating domestic development and opening up to the outside world, promoting the coordination between productive forces and production relations, and the economic base and the superstructure, and coordinating all aspects of economic, political, and cultural construction. *Sustainable development* means promoting harmony between man and nature, achieving coordination between economic development, and population, resources, and environment, adhering to the civilized development path of productive development, affluent life, and good ecology, and ensuring sustainable development from generation to generation (Editorial Team of A Brief History of the Communist Party of China, 2021).

If we compare Jiang Zemin and Hu Jintao, we can observe some differences in their understanding and practice of statecraft. Below are some of the major differences:

> Firstly, different focus on development. During Jiang's tenure, Chinese policies emphasized economic construction and national economic modernization, pursuing enhanced national economic strength, with a focus on economic growth. In contrast, Hu Jintao placed more emphasis on social fairness and improving people's livelihoods, proposing the concept of "building and sharing together," focusing on social issues, ensuring that all people could share the growth results of national wealth.

Secondly, emphasis on sustainable development. Although Jiang Zemin also paid attention to environmental issues, he relatively less emphasized environmental protection and ecological civilization, focusing more on economic construction. In contrast, Hu emphasized the importance of environmental protection and sustainable development, proposing the concept of building an ecological civilization and adopting a series of policies to promote environmental protection and sustainable development.

Thirdly, handling political systems and social issues: During Jiang's tenure, there was relatively more emphasis on political stability and social control, adopting relatively stringent measures on some social issues to maintain national stability. Hu, instead, advocated social harmony, paid more attention to handling social issues, adopted a series of policies to reduce poverty, improve education and medical levels, emphasizing social fairness and improving people's livelihoods.

In summary, the eras of Deng Xiaoping and Jiang Zemin focused more on economic growth and the accumulation of economic strength, while the eras of Hu Jintao and Xi Jinping focused more on the transformation of economic strength. Hu Jintao emphasized the transformation of economic strength toward domestic aspects such as social harmony and environmental protection, while Xi Jinping focused on both domestic and international transformations, such as the external "Belt and Road Initiative" and the domestic "Three-Year Poverty Alleviation" and "Common Prosperity".

In many aspects, Hu Jintao's approach lies somewhere between that of Deng Xiaoping and Xi Jinping. Once Xi Jinping assumed power, he began to implement a Marxist-Developmentalist synthesis in his approach to economic statecraft.

Notes

1 Key characteristics and goals of developmentalism include:

1. Economic Growth and Development: The primary objective is to achieve rapid and sustainable economic growth. This often involves significant investment in infrastructure, industry, and technology to modernize the economy.
2. State-Led Initiatives: Governments play a proactive role in guiding the economy. This can include strategic planning, directing investment in key sectors, and sometimes directly managing certain industries or resources.
3. Industrialization: A major focus is often on developing a strong industrial base. This can involve moving away from an economy based primarily on agriculture or raw material exports to one that is more diversified and industrialized.
4. Protectionism and Trade Policy: Developmentalism may involve protecting nascent industries through tariffs and other trade barriers until they are competitive internationally. However, this aspect can vary depending on the specific strategies of a country.

5 Improving Living Standards: Alongside economic growth, there's often an emphasis on improving the general living standards of the population, including reducing poverty and increasing access to education and healthcare.

In contrast to more laissez-faire or market-driven economic models, developmentalism relies on active government intervention and strategic planning to steer national economic development. This approach has been particularly prevalent in many East Asian economies, like South Korea and Taiwan, especially in the post-World War II era.

The above discussion is based on a conversation with OpenAI's ChatGPT, where ChatGPT provided information and analysis based on its training data. The conversation took place on November 24, 2023.

2 The "Two Newspapers and One Magazine" refers to two newspapers and one magazine in Mainland China that were the most authoritative and influential during and for a period after the Cultural Revolution. These three media outlets typically refer to the People's Daily (《人民日报》), the PLA Daily (《解放军报》), and the Red Flag magazine (later renamed "Seeking Truth" or《求是》).

3 The outbreak of SARS occurred toward the end of 2002 and into 2003. This epidemic was first identified in November 2002 in Guangdong Province, China. It then rapidly spread globally, particularly peaking in the spring of 2003. By July 2003, the World Health Organization (WHO) declared that the SARS epidemic was largely contained.

Reference List

Angus, M. (2007) *Development Centre Studies Chinese Economic Performance in the Long Run, 960–2030 AD, Second Edition, Revised and Updated.* Paris: OECD Publishing.

Bottelier, P. (2018) *Economic Policy Making in China (1949–2016): The Role of Economists.* London: Routledge.

China News. (2008) *The Backstory of Deng Xiaoping's 'Black Cat, White Cat Theory': Originally a Sichuan Colloquialism* [China News] 17 December. Available at: http://www.chinanews.com.cn/cul/news/2008/12-17/1490780.shtml

Editorial Team of a Brief History of the Communist Party of China. (2021). *A Brief History of the Communist Party of China.* Beijing: People's Publishing House. Available at: https://article.xuexi.cn/articles/pdf/index.html?art_id=16572413292965867289&study_style_id=feeds_wm_list&pid=2552501410944284 6&ptype=75&source=share&share_to=wx_single

Editorial Team of the Economic History of China. (2019) *Economic History of China.* Beijing: Higher Education Press.

Hu, J. T. (2016) "Speech at a Presentation on the Study of Selected Works of Jiang Zemin", *Selected Works of Hu Jintao.* Beijing: People's Publishing House.

Li, Q. G. (2022) *How Did the Important Thought of Three Represents Come into Being?* [Study Times] 2 December.

Mao, Z. D. (1977) *Selected Works of Mao Zedong (Volume 5).* Beijing: People's Publishing House.

Mao, Z. D. (2002) "Don't Strike Out on All Sides", *Selected Works of Mao Zedong.* Beijing: CPC Central Party School Publishing House.

National Bureau of Statistics. (1979) *Summary of National Economic Statistics for the 30 Years after the Founding of the People's Republic of China (1949–1978).*

News of the Communist Party of China. (2023) *What Is the Significance of the Great Debate on the Criterion of Truth?* Available at: http://cpc.people.com.cn/GB/64156/64157/4418445.html (Accessed: November 25, 2023)

Study Times. (2020) *Chen Yun and His Financial Work in Resisting America and Aiding Korea* [Study Times] 23 October. Available at: http://dangshi.people.com.cn/n1/2020/1023/c85037-31902907.html

Wu, X. B. (2013) *Successive Economic Changes Gain and Lose*. Hangzhou: Zhejiang University Press.

Xie, Y. X. (2002) *A History of Contemporary Chinese Diplomacy*. Beijing: China Youth Publishing House.

3 Hu Jintao's Time

The Origin of China's New Economic Statecraft

Hu Jintao was a moderate, cautious, and low-profile president. He was not ambitious in exerting China's global influence, showing greater interest in domestic issues. However, during his presidency, China experienced rapid growth, especially economically. The year 2008 was a watershed moment for both the world and China's rise. Hu and his comrades faced an unprecedented historical opportunity to catapult China onto the world's center stage.

Hu and his ministers introduced new initiatives in economic statecraft focused on global economic governance, achieving very limited successes. Hu's tenure laid the groundwork for the emergence of China's new economic statecraft under Xi Jinping's leadership.

3.1 Rise of China's Economy

During Hu Jintao's tenure, China's GDP grew from being ranked 6th in 2002 to 2nd in 2010, surpassing Japan. The GDP increased from 1.47 trillion USD in 2002 to 8.23 trillion USD, a more than fivefold increase within a decade. In terms of trade, China moved from 6th place in 2002 to 1st in 2012, becoming the world's largest trading nation. Regarding FDI inflow, China was ranked 2nd globally. As for FDI outflow, China was ranked 3rd in 2012, only behind the United States and Germany.

It indeed remains a puzzle how China achieved its economic rise in such a short period of time. During Hu Jintao's era, China achieved double-digit economic growth annually, primarily benefiting from the following economic policies and strategies:

1 Continuous Advancement of Reform and Opening-up Policies: During Hu Jintao's term, the policies of reform and opening up were continuously advanced, particularly more profound reforms in areas such as finance, state-owned enterprises, and land use.
2 Investment-Driven Economic Growth: During this period, China's infrastructure construction and real estate industry developed rapidly.

DOI: 10.4324/9781003270379-4

A significant amount of investment was poured into these areas, promoting rapid economic growth.

3 Export-Oriented Economic Strategy: In Hu Jintao's era, China maintained its position as the world's factory, exporting a vast amount of low-cost goods worldwide, which drove economic growth.
4 Emphasis on Innovation and Education: Under Hu Jintao's leadership, China began to place more emphasis on innovation and education, striving to improve the overall quality of its citizens and the country's capabilities in scientific and technological innovation.

So, in many ways, Hu Jintao's economic statecraft was a continuation of the economic growth model established by Deng Xiaoping and Jiang Zemin. That being said, Hu Jintao encountered challenges that his predecessors had not, such as the SARS outbreak and the Global Financial Crisis of 2008. These events significantly shaped Hu's approach to developmentalist economic statecraft.

3.2 Hu Jintao's Developmentalist Economic Statecraft

The first major challenge that Hu had to face was SARS in 2003. That largely shaped his 10-year term. At the end of August and the beginning of September 2003, during his inspection in Jiangxi, Hu Jintao proposed the concept of the "Scientific Development View", emphasizing the need to firmly establish a scientific approach to coordinated, comprehensive, and sustainable development. In 2005, Hu Jintao put forward the ideas of a "Harmonious Society and Harmonious World". In 2006, he advocated for "Transforming the Mode of Economic Development to Achieve Rapid and Sound Economic Growth".

The year 2008 was the most challenging year for Hu Jintao's statecraft. That year saw several significant events: the Wenchuan earthquake in May, the Beijing Olympics in August, and the global financial crisis in October, during which Hu Jintao called for "Being Prepared to Respond to Difficult Situations" (Hu, 2016c).

In the context of the Global Financial Crisis, China's foreign trade exports experienced negative growth for two consecutive months in November and December 2008. Premier Wen Jiabao candidly stated at the annual meeting of the Davos World Economic Forum, "The main problems (of the Chinese economy) are: a significant contraction in external demand, overcapacity in some industries, difficulties in enterprise production and operation, an increase in urban unemployment, and obviously increased downward pressure on the economy" (China Government Website, 2009).

In parallel, Hu Jintao proposed that, "for the foreseeable future, diplomatic efforts should prioritize effectively responding to the international financial crisis and supporting sustained, stable economic growth.

These efforts should focus on safeguarding economic development, improving people's livelihoods, and maintaining stability, while actively strategizing for these goals. We need to strengthen economic diplomacy, actively participate in international cooperation to respond to the impact of the international financial crisis, promote the recovery of world economic growth, and actively advance our country's practical cooperation with various countries…" (Hu, 2016d).

During Hu Jintao's era, the guiding ideology behind his economic statecraft was anchored in the belief that "our country would, for a considerable time, remain in the initial stage of socialism. Facing fierce international competition in comprehensive national strength, we must prioritize economic construction, firmly seize and utilize the period of important strategic opportunity, and vigorously liberate and develop the social productive forces. This approach is strategically significant for a large developing country like ours, as it accelerates our journey toward modernization" (Hu, 2016b).

In many ways, Hu Jintao's economic statecraft was still that of a developing country, emphasizing economic growth. For Hu Jintao, the primary task of China's diplomacy during the Global Financial Crisis was to support China's economic growth. In other words, China's economic statecraft aimed to use diplomacy in the service of its economy. This approach is a salient feature of the economic statecraft of developing countries.

The former US Secretary of Treasury Henry Paulson recalled, "When President Bush asked President Hu what worried him the most, Hu replied that it was the annual creation of 25 million job opportunities". In Paulson's analysis, "Chinese leaders place stability above everything, which means that a strong economy is essential. Accordingly, China needs more market-oriented reforms and a mutually beneficial relationship with its most important trading partner, the United States. Essentially, the Communist Party has made an agreement with the people to exchange prosperity for long-term political power. Chinese leaders root their credibility among the populace in economic opportunities, job creation, and continuously improving living standards. These elements act like glue, holding the system together. However, China's continued success has raised the people's expectations. As social pressures increase, these expectations become increasingly difficult to meet. These pressures include poor air and water quality, as well as distressing income disparities" (Paulson, 2016).

In 2009, the youth unemployment rate in China was notably high, with nearly 2 million college graduates unable to find jobs. This represented about 32% of the 6.1 million graduates that year. The high unemployment rate among youth during this period can be attributed to several factors, including structural mismatches between the skills possessed by graduates and those demanded by the labor market. This issue was compounded by the economic conditions of the time, which made it particularly challenging for young people, especially those from less prestigious universities, to secure quality employment. This is why Hu Jintao's economic statecraft, focused on economic growth, embodies a developmentalist approach.

3.3 Hu Jintao's Efforts in Translating China's Wealth to Global Influence

The most significant transformation of wealth into power during Hu Jintao's tenure was the enhancement of global economic governance mechanisms and the international financial system. After the outbreak of the financial crisis in 2008, until stepping down in 2012, Hu Jintao continually pushed for the reform of global governance. Hu Jintao proposed at the Central Economic Work Conference in 2010 that it is necessary to accurately grasp the characteristics of the world economic governance mechanism entering a period of transformation, striving to enhance our country's ability to participate in and guide this process (Hu, 2016a).

Hu Jintao's keen interest in reforming the global economic governance system stems from the response to the Global Financial Crisis. The global financial crisis of 2008 exposed numerous weaknesses and problems in the current international financial system and global economic governance structure. As the leader of China, Hu Jintao understood that reforming the global economic governance system was an effective way to address and prevent similar crises.

Hu Jintao fully understood that by actively participating in the reform of the global economic governance system, China could play a greater role in shaping international economic policies and rules, thereby enhancing its status and influence in global economic governance.

But Hu's reform of global governance was not driven by personal ambition. It was more about meeting China's domestic needs, especially in terms of economic development. Hu Jintao's tenure highlighted the dialectical relationship between wealth and power.

From the wealth perspective, China's economic base was still relatively weak, necessitating that economic diplomacy serve development. Hu Jintao proposed that the key to solving China's problems lay in relying on its own development.

From the power perspective, the greatest ambition in transforming wealth into power during Hu Jintao's term was the promotion of global economic governance mechanisms and the international financial system. Zhou Xiaochuan, the then Chinese central bank governor, proposed a "super-sovereign international reserve currency", reflecting China's aspirations and dissatisfaction with the US dollar hegemony. Chen Deming, the then Chinese Minister of Commerce, also advanced rule reconstruction in response to the global financial crisis, later summarized in his book "Economic Crisis and Rule Reconstruction" (Chen, 2014). After the outbreak of the financial crisis in 2008, and until stepping down in 2012, Hu Jintao continuously advocated for the reform of global governance.

However, Hu's economic statecraft achieved very limited success, leading to frustrations among Chinese policy elites after his tenure. This paved the way for Xi Jinping's new approach to economic statecraft.

Below is an initial assessment of Hu's economic statecraft initiatives:

> Firstly on trade. In 2001, one event was China, the world's largest developing country, joining the World Trade Organization, and the other was placing development issues at the core of the trade field for the first time in the history of multilateral trade negotiations, naming the new round of multilateral trade negotiations the Development Agenda. There is nothing more historically significant than the coincidence of these two events.
>
> (Chai, 2015)

As China's economic strength grew and its trade volume continuously expanded, in 2008, China was invited to join the core group of the Doha Round negotiations, the Group of 7 (G7), along with Brazil, India, and the traditional powers of the US, the European Communities, Japan, and Australia. This invitation marked a shift in the history of multilateral trade, which had been dominated by the Group of 4 (the US, the EC, Japan, and Canada). Reuters commented at the time that China had finally moved to the forefront, taking a seat at the main table and changing the power dynamics of the negotiations. Some even jokingly referred to China as the "elephant in the green room" (Note: "Green room" meetings refer to ministerial/ambassador-level consultations convened by the Director-General of the WTO in their office) (Chai, 2015).

However, China had not assumed leadership in the global economy through the Doha Round multilateral trade negotiations that started in 2001, and it did not respond effectively when the United States shifted focus from Doha to regional and bilateral trade talks in 2004 and afterward. Thus far in its modern history, China has not realized global economic leadership, despite its clear position as the world's largest beneficiary of an open multilateral trading system (Zhang and Keith, 2017).

For many, it remains a puzzle why China is reluctant or ineffectual in its exercise of firmer leadership in the world trading system. One possible explanation is that Chinese leaders believed that it took time before China could grasp the World Trade Organization (WTO) rules since China used to perceive and claim itself as a new member who only joined in 2001. For example, before assuming his ambassadorial position in January 2002, the first Chinese Ambassador received instruction from Beijing to not hinder nor lead the WTO negotiations in Geneva (Phoenix Info, 2016). This "good student" mentality did not change until the 2008 Global Financial Crisis, when China realized it was indeed time to assert its leadership in the global trade talks. However, non-compromise between the United States and India, among other factors, dashed hopes of concluding the Doha Round successfully.

China's inability to define for itself a leading position in the global economy is further illustrated, from the Chinese perspective, by its failure thus far to achieve so-called Market Economy Status (MES). China believed that the MES should be granted without objection 15 years after China's accession to the WTO, which occurred in 2001. The United States and the EU, at least until now, seem to believe otherwise (Gary and Cathleen, 2015).

In July 2008, the World Trade Organization's Doha Round of negotiations, involving a small group of ministers, ended once again without any results. The global trade sector was immersed in extreme disappointment. During the meeting where Pascal Lamy announced the breakdown of the negotiations, the EU's Commissioner for agriculture was choked up several times while speaking (Chai, 2015). The failure of the 2008 WTO Ministerial meeting also served as a wake-up call for Chen Deming, the Chinese Minister of Commerce. He delved deeper into these reflections in his book "Economic Crisis and Rule Reconstruction" (Chen, 2014). As a key policy figure under Hu Jintao's leadership, Chen believed in the necessity of reforming the existing rules of the global economic system.

Secondly on finance.

Finance is the second origin of the Chinese perspective on economic statecraft. For example, in 2009 during the peak of the financial crisis, the Chinese central bank governor Zhou Xiaochuan wrote an article titled "Reform the International Monetary System", proposing for a "super-sovereign international reserve currency", which reflected China's aspirations and dissatisfaction with the US dollar hegemony (Zhou, 2009).

For Zhou Xiaochuan, an international reserve currency should first be anchored to a stable benchmark and issued according to a clear set of rules, therefore to ensure orderly supply; second, its supply should be flexible enough to allow timely adjustment according to the changing demand; third, such adjustments should be disconnected from economic conditions and sovereign interests of any single country. The outbreak of the Global Financial Crisis and its spillover to the entire world reflect the inherent vulnerabilities and systemic risks in the existing international monetary system. Zhou believes that the desirable goal of reforming the international monetary system is to create an international reserve currency that is disconnected from individual nations and is able to remain stable in the long run, thus removing the inherent deficiencies caused by using credit-based national currencies (Zhou, 2009).

Zhou proposed replacing the US dollar with a super-sovereign international reserve currency as the world's reserve currency. He suggested that Keynes's "Bancor", introduced during the Bretton Woods Conference, was a more farsighted concept. This foresight, according to Zhou, is evidenced by the collapse of the Bretton Woods system, which relied on the approach proposed by Harry White (Zhou, 2009).

Amidst the financial crisis, Zhou Xiaochuan's article sent shockwaves around the world and was widely regarded as China's first open challenge to the international status of the US dollar (Drezner, 2009). It also marked a significant debut for China on the international financial diplomacy stage, representing the first time China systematically expressed its dissatisfaction with the existing international financial order. In fact, just days before Zhou Xiaochuan's article was published, Russia had already put forward a similar proposition. However, there was no international response to Russia's suggestion until Zhou Xiaochuan made his proposal, at which point the international community reacted as if a pot of oil had exploded. Zhou Xiaochuan's article received positive responses from emerging countries such as Russia, Brazil, India, Argentina, and Indonesia, demonstrating the appeal of China's financial diplomacy (Li, 2015).

Furthermore, to acknowledge the significance of China's financial power, France, the rotating president of the G20 summit in 2011, specifically hosted a seminar on "Reforming the International Monetary System" in Nanjing, China. This seminar gathered finance ministers, central bank governors from the G20 and related countries, representatives of international organizations, and key scholars in the fields of international economics and currency.

However, China's financial diplomacy in reforming the international monetary system has achieved very limited success. Most Western countries have expressed opposition to China's suggestion to switch reserve currencies. The United States reacted swiftly and strongly, with President Obama responding promptly to Zhou Xiaochuan's suggestion by stating that there is no need to create a new global currency. Although the European Union supports a greater role for emerging countries, it is less enthusiastic about changing the reserve currency. Joaquín Almunia, the EU Commissioner for Economic and Monetary Affairs, said in an interview that he did not see a significant structural change in the dollar's role as a major reserve currency today. After a meeting at the European Commission, Almunia remarked, "Everyone believes that the current global reserve currency, the dollar, is still here and will remain so for a long time". Australian Prime Minister Kevin Rudd also expressed a similar sentiment during his visit to the United States, stating in Washington that the dollar's status as a reserve currency is indisputable (Jiemian News, 2009). As a result, the US dollar remains the world's dominant reserve currency.

Third, on energy, China is deeply and increasingly concerned about potential disruptions to its sea lanes of economic supply, especially the narrow passage of the Malacca Strait, which from Beijing's perspective could be easily blockaded to the detriment of China's economic development and security. Accordingly, China is seeking to lock up sources of supply and create alternate routes of delivery that require its innovative use of channels of investment not beholden to the West (Zhang and Keith, 2017).

From 2002 to 2012, the most notable achievement in Sino-Russian energy diplomacy was the completion of the China-Russia crude oil pipeline. This pipeline is part of the "East Siberia-Pacific Ocean Pipeline" system, aimed at exporting Russian crude oil to the Asia-Pacific market.

Negotiations for the China-Russia crude oil pipeline began in 1997 but progressed slowly due to various reasons. In 2009, China and Russia signed an agreement in which China provided a $25 billion loan to Russia. In exchange, starting from 2011, China would import 15 million tons of oil annually from Russia over a 20-year period. As part of this agreement, it was decided to lay a pipeline from Skovorodino in Russia to Daqing in China. This pipeline was completed on September 27, 2010. Since January 1, 2011, it has been transporting 300,000 barrels of oil per day. This is known as the "loan-for-oil" project.

Between 2002 and 2012, the most prominent achievement in China's energy diplomacy with Central Asia was the construction of the China-Central Asia natural gas pipeline. The initial intention behind building the China-Central Asia natural gas pipeline was to extend the existing China-Kazakhstan oil pipeline. The actual construction of the natural gas pipeline has provided China with a steady supply of natural gas and has spurred economic development in Central Asian countries. Its significance for China and the Central Asian countries is similar to that of the China-Russia crude oil pipeline project (Wu, 2015).

Fourth, on technology, China has become even more deeply frustrated with the persistent arms embargo and export controls of dual-use products imposed by the Western world. Some of these measures date from normalization and have evolved; that evolution was affected by the "Tiananmen Incident" on June 4, 1989 (Zhang and Keith, 2017).

In response, China started to implement the Innovation-Driven Development Strategy (IDDS) in 2006. The IDDS is built around the idea that a very specific wave of technological change is beginning. The configuration of this wave of technological change thus gives increasingly a definite form to policy. It also means that, in the IDDS, the opportunity to move directly to the technological frontier and surpass other economies is no longer a wished-for feature of a few random sectors but rather a fundamental feature of the current global moment. Increasingly, Chinese industrial policy is based on the idea that China has a once-in-a-lifetime opportunity to get in on the ground floor of a technological revolution and vault into the leading ranks of economic and technological powers (Naughton, 2021).

In summary, Hu Jintao's economic statecraft yielded mixed results. While there were successes, most achievements were only partially realized, whether in the realm of WTO leadership or in efforts to reform the international monetary system.

Hu Jintao's tenure witnessed China's rapid economic ascent. However, this period was also marked by a significant dilemma: despite growing economic strengths, China faced an increasingly challenging international environment, characterized by heightened pushback and skepticism about its global role. This predicament significantly shaped the economic statecraft of both Hu Jintao and his successor. In response, Hu initiated economic statecraft initiatives focused on reforming global economic governance, leveraging China's burgeoning economic capabilities. However, these efforts were far from complete, leading to frustration among Chinese policy elites and setting the stage for Xi Jinping's new approach to economic statecraft.

Reference List

Chai, X. L. (2015) "the WTO", in Zhang, X. T. and Wang, H. Y., co-eds, *Chinese Economic Diplomacy: The PRC's Growing International Influence in the 21st Century*. London: ACA Publishing Ltd.

Chen, D. M. (2014) *The Economic Crisis and the Restructuring of Rules*. Beijing: The Commercial Press.

China Government Website. (2009) *Premier Wen Jiabao Attended the World Economic Forum Annual Meeting and Delivered a Special Speech*. 29 January. Available at: https://www.gov.cn/ldhd/2009-01/29/content_1216758.htm

Drezner, D. W. (2009) "Bad Debts: Assessing China's Financial Influence in Great Power Politics", *International Security*. 34(2), p. 39.

Gary, C. H., and Cathleen, C. (2015) *Looming US-China Trade Battles?: Market Economy Status* [Part II] 9 March, Peterson Institute. Available at: https://piie.com/blogs/trade-investment-policy-watch/looming-us-china-trade-battles-market-economy-status-part-ii.

Hu, J. T. (2016a) "Accurately Grasp the New Characteristics of World Economic Development: Speech at the Central Economic Work Conference", *Selected Works of Hu Jintao (Volume 3)*. Beijing: People's Publishing House.

Hu, J. T. (2016b) "Accurately Grasp the Profound Connotation and Basic Requirements of the Scientific Outlook on Development – Speech at the Central Symposium on Population, Resources and Environment Work", *Selected Works of Hu Jintao (Volume 2)*. Beijing: People's Publishing House.

Hu, J. T. (2016c) "Be Prepared for Difficult Situations", *Selected Works of Hu Jintao (Volume 3)*. Beijing: People's Publishing House.

Hu, J. T. (2016d) "Coordinating the Two Overall Situations at Home and Abroad: Speech at the 11th Meeting of Diplomatic Envoys Abroad", *Selected Works of Hu Jintao (Volume 3)*. Beijing: People's Publishing House.

Jiemian News. (2009) *Zhou Xiaochuan's 'Super-sovereign' Currency is Opposed by the West* [in Chinese] 30 March. Available at: https://finance.sina.cn/sa/2009-03-30/detail-ikknscsi7080896.d.html?from=wap

Li, W. (2015) "Fiscal and Financial Diplomacy", in Zhang, X. T. and Wang, H. Y., co-eds, *Chinese Economic Diplomacy: The PRC's Growing International Influence in the 21st Century*. London: ACA Publishing Ltd.

Naughton, B. (2021) *The Rise of China's Industrial Policy, 1978 to 2020*. Mexico City: Universidad Nacional Autónoma de México.

Paulson, H. M. J. (2016) Dealing with China: An Insider Unmasks the New Economic Superpower (in Chinese). Translated by Wang, Y. G., Zhu, Y., Zhu, Q. W., and Wang, H. Hongkong: The Chinese University Press.

Phoenix Info, (2016) *Is the WTO Still Useful? The First Chinese Ambassador Explains How China Managed to be Part of the Core Decision-Making* [in Chinese] 11 December. Available at: http://www.ccg.org.cn/archives/30254

Wu, J. (2015) "Energy Diplomacy", in Zhang, X. T. and Wang, H. Y., co-eds, *Chinese Economic Diplomacy: The PRC's Growing International Influence in the 21st Century*. London: ACA Publishing Ltd.

Zhang, X. T., and Keith, J. (2017) *"From Wealth to Power: China's New Economic Statecraft". The Washington Quarterly* [Spring], p. 189.

Zhou, X. C. (2009) *Reflections on the Reform of International Monetary System* [in Chinese], People's Bank of China, 23 March. Available at: http://www.pbc.gov.cn/hanglingdao/128697/128719/128772/825742/index.html.

4 Xi Jinping's New Economic Statecraft (2012–2017)

Marxist-Developmentalist Synthesis Based on Confucius-Mencius Philosophy

President Xi Jinping has championed China's new economic statecraft, exemplified by numerous ambitious projects such as the Belt and Road Initiative (BRI), the Asian Infrastructure Investment Bank (AIIB), Bilateral Investment Treaties (BITs) with the EU and the USA, and the Regional Comprehensive Economic Partnership (RCEP). Xi is the first Chinese leader since Mao Zedong to actively seek to transform China's accumulated national wealth into a prominent position on the world stage.

He had strong motivations to do that. After assuming office, Xi Jinping faced significant responsibilities, with the accumulated issues from previous generations of leaders weighing on him alone. He is dedicated to addressing a series of governance problems in China that have persisted since the era of Deng Xiaoping.

Xi's worldview is rooted in a fearless, Marxist perspective. Alongside his Politburo colleagues, including the new Premier Li Keqiang and Vice Premier Wang Yang, he sought transformative changes. Under Xi's leadership, Li Keqiang's landmark initiative was the establishment of the Free Trade Zones (FTZs) and the supply-side structural reform. Vice Premier Wang Yang notably contributed to this direction by playing a key role in negotiating the Bilateral Investment Treaty with the United States. During Xi's first term (2012–2017), there appeared to be a consensus within the Communist Party of China (CPC) toward further reform and opening-up. In other words, within the CPC's Marxist political ideological framework, economic liberalism remained a vibrant force.

For Xi Jinping, he had a higher political pursuit – to achieve China's Great Rejuvenation. On November 29, 2012, shortly after the closing of the 18th National Congress of the CPC, Xi Jinping, along with members of the Politburo Standing Committee including Li Keqiang, Zhang Dejiang, Yu Zhengsheng, Liu Yunshan, Wang Qishan, and Zhang Gaoli, visited the "Road to Revival" exhibition at the National Museum. Through this exhibition, they reviewed the arduous journey of the Chinese nation since modern times and emphasized the historical mission of realizing the great rejuvenation of the Chinese nation and the Chinese Dream.

DOI: 10.4324/9781003270379-5

When Xi Jinping introduced a new type of economic statecraft with the BRI, he drew upon two sources that he critiqued: the ancient Chinese Confucius-Mencius philosophy coupled with the Tribute System, and the more contemporary American Marshall Plan. The former has been a part of Chinese culture for over two millennia, while the latter represents a relatively recent development. Both sources were inspirational yet problematic. For Xi and his colleagues, critically evaluating both the Tribute System and the Marshall Plan was essential in shaping China's newly emerging economic statecraft (CGTN, 2019).

To pursue China's Great Rejuvenation, Xi started to implement the "Major-Country Diplomacy" with Chinese characteristics ("中国特色大国外交"). In 2014, Xi Jinping first proposed at the Central Foreign Affairs Work Conference that China must have its own characteristic major-country diplomacy, which should embody distinctive Chinese features, Chinese style, and Chinese grandeur in its foreign affairs work. In 2017, Xi explicitly stated in the report of the 19th National Congress of the Communist Party the need to "comprehensively advance China's characteristic major-country diplomacy", and incorporated it into the guiding ideology and strategic deployment for adhering to and developing socialism with Chinese characteristics in the new era (Wang, 2022).

Within the framework of China's Major-Country Diplomacy, 2013, marked a new beginning for China's economic statecraft. For over 30 years since 1978, China's diplomacy has primarily served economic development. However, with the rapidly evolving global context and China's more proactive role in international affairs, the nation has increasingly utilized economic statecraft to transform its national wealth into global influence.

Since Xi's new leadership took office, China has implemented a series of major economic diplomacy initiatives, such as the "BRI", "Two Corridors and Two Banks",[1] "High-speed Rail Diplomacy",[2] and "Nuclear Energy Diplomacy".[3] Each of these initiatives involves major financial commitments and covers multiple countries and regions (see Table 4.1 for details). Economic diplomacy is becoming an increasingly important tool for China to achieve its great power ambitions.

In 2010, China's GDP surpassed that of Japan, making it the world's second-largest economy. China has become a major economic power with global influence. The development of China is not only that of a large-scale country but also that of a developing country. For Chinese policy elites, how to better transform the comprehensive strength of a major country into its diplomatic capabilities has become a significant issue that concerns both the nation's destiny and the fate of humanity (Wang, 2017).

China's peaceful development faces a series of dilemmas. First is the security dilemma: China needs peaceful development, but national security is challenged by issues of sovereignty and territorial disputes, including the South China Sea dispute, the East China Sea dispute, and the India-China

Table 4.1 List of regions, sectors, and financial commitments covered by China's new economic diplomacy initiatives

	Belt and Road	*Two corridors and two banks*	*High-speed rail diplomacy*	*Nuclear energy diplomacy*
Countries and Regions Covered	The Silk Road Economic Belt mainly involves Central Asia, West Asia, and Central and Eastern Europe, including countries such as Russia, Kazakhstan, Russia, Iran, and Saudi Arabia. The 21st-century Maritime Silk Road mainly involves Southeast Asia, South Asia, West Asia, and North Africa, with involvement from Indonesia, Thailand, Bangladesh, India, Pakistan, Oman, Kenya, and Egypt.	The Bangladesh-China-India-Myanmar (BCIM) Economic Corridor mainly involves South Asia, including India, Myanmar, and Bangladesh. The China-Pakistan Economic Corridor (CPEC) mainly involves Pakistan. The Asian Infrastructure Investment Bank (AIIB) is primarily for Asia, focusing on developing countries in the continent. The New Development Bank (NDB) supports infrastructure construction in member and related countries and the expansion of overseas interests; it has set up a Contingency Reserve Arrangement (CRA) to provide assistance funding to members in the event of financial emergencies, such as capital flight or debt crises.	China's "high-speed rail diplomacy" covers East Asia, South Asia, Southeast Asia, Central Asia, West Asia, Central and Eastern Europe, the Americas, and Africa, including Russia, the United States, the United Kingdom, Brazil, Venezuela, Vietnam, Myanmar, India, Pakistan, Iran, Thailand, Turkey, Saudi Arabia, Kenya, and certain Central and Eastern European countries.	China's "nuclear energy diplomacy" covers Europe and North America, including the United States, France, the United Kingdom, and Romania.
Sectors	Energy, finance, investment, trade, communications, transportation, agriculture	Critical projects, infrastructure, energy and resources, agriculture and water resources, and information and communication	Transportation	Energy

Source: Made by the author.

border dispute. Second is the development dilemma: China's domestic economy needs upgrading and rejuvenation due to insufficient economic driving forces, yet China also faces the task of safeguarding its expanding overseas interests. While China's domestic economic growth is slowing down and its economic development model is in a transitional and challenging phase, it urgently needs to rely on its economic strength to provide material support for expanding international influence. These issues constitute the twin dilemmas of security and development for China, leading to contradictions between the deepening global interdependence and China's need to strengthen strategic autonomy, and between China's narrative of "major country responsibilities" and its status and power as a developing country. Resolving these two major dilemmas is necessary (Wang, 2017).

4.1 Xi Jinping's New Economic Statecraft (2012–2017): Marxist-Developmentalist Synthesis Based on Confucius-Mencius Philosophy

Xi Jinping's economic statecraft is largely a synthesis of the developmentalist and Marxist approaches, combined with China's classic Confucian philosophy. To a large extent, Xi Jinping's economic statecraft combines the approaches of Mao Zedong and Deng Xiaoping.

4.1.1 Xi Jinping's Developmentalist Approach to Economic Statecraft

Unlike America, China's economic statecraft has traditionally been developmentalist. Even during Xi Jinping's tenure, the focus of China's economic statecraft remains heavily on economic development. In other words, in China's approach to economic statecraft, power is utilized to generate wealth, and wealth is leveraged to increase power. This creates a continuous dialectic interaction between wealth and power.

Against this background, Xi Jinping proposed the BRI. He pointed out that the construction of the "Belt and Road" is a major strategic move for China to expand its opening-up to the outside world and is the top-level design of its economic diplomacy. It serves as the master plan for China's external opening-up and cooperation for a considerable period in the future, and it is also China's proactive approach in promoting the reform of the global governance system (Zhong, 2017).

Originally envisioned as summit deliverables during his visits to Kazakhstan and Indonesia, Xi Jinping rapidly transformed the BRI into the most significant economic statecraft initiative of his tenure. The BRI was evidently President Xi's favored project. It had not existed on any think tank's desk, nor was it mentioned. Even in a significant policy speech delivered by then-Foreign Minister Wang Yi in June 2013, this concept was absent (Wang, 2013a). It is said that President Xi greatly enjoyed his trip to Kazakhstan and was impressed by the enthusiasm in Kazakhstan for his idea of the Silk Road Economic Belt.

The BRI has a dual purpose. On one hand, it aims to foster domestic economic growth. On the other hand, it is designed to convert China's economic strengths into global influence. These two purposes reinforce each other. The Chinese policy elites are fully aware that China's weight in the world economy and global governance has risen rapidly, but the issue of being a large yet not strong economy remains prominent. The transformation of China's economic strength into international institutional power still requires strenuous effort. China's opening-up has entered a more balanced stage of both bringing in and going out, but the systems and forces supporting high-level opening-up and large-scale outward expansion still appear weak (Publicity Department of the Communist Party of China, 2016, p. 135).

To establish an open development concept, it is necessary to conform to the trend of China's economy deeply integrating into the world economy. This involves pursuing a mutually beneficial and win-win open strategy, maintaining a balance between domestic and foreign demands, balancing imports and exports, giving equal importance to both attracting investment and going global, and concurrently focusing on attracting capital, technology, and intelligence. It's about developing a higher-level open economy, actively participating in global economic governance and the provision of public goods, enhancing China's institutional say in global economic governance, and building a broad community of shared interests (Publicity Department of the Communist Party of China, 2016, pp. 135–136).

So, the first characteristic of Xi Jinping's economic statecraft is developmentalism. In many ways, Xi's economic statecraft, particularly during his first term (2012–2017), represents a continuation of the developmentalism that began in China with Deng Xiaoping.

Xi Jinping's developmentalist economic statecraft is linked to the state of the domestic economy. China's economic growth – based on fixed asset investment, the main engine of wealth creation – has decelerated since 2014 and entered into a "new normal", to use a popular term. This new phase represents a downshifting from a high-speed growth pattern of 1992–2012 toward a sustainable, mid- to high-speed growth rate with higher efficiency and lower costs. There is considerable debate about the degree to which China can succeed in this economic restructuring. The economic slowdown has spurred China's ambitious agenda of economic statecraft and posed main challenges, which significantly constrain the translation of China's wealth into power and global influence (Zhang and Keith, 2017). This is why President Xi and his colleagues vigorously promoted economic statecraft projects like the BRI to enhance the conversion of wealth into power. In many ways, the economic slowdown and overcapacity spurred Chinese leaders to develop innovative economic statecraft tools to foster economic growth and translate it into global influence.

"New Normal" is a term coined by Xi Jinping and his economic advisors in May 2014 (People, 2014). It represents a judgment made through a comprehensive analysis of the world economy's long cycle, along with the stage-specific characteristics of China's development and their interactions, indicating that China's economic development has entered a new phase (Xi, 2017, p. 239).

The Chinese leadership is convinced that the future evolution of China's economy is an "L" shape, featuring sluggish aggregate demands and overproduction. It is over a period, rather than one or two years, that China's economy will grow in an L-Shape (Gong et al., 2016). This may reflect the global context of a B-phase, as suggested by the Chinese Academy of Governance and Yao et al. It is based on the analysis of long cycles of the world economy and the characteristics of China's development stage, as well as the mutual interactions between these two factors, that the Chinese leadership believes China's economy will go through a relatively long period of L-Shaped growth, and has therefore decided to implement "supply-side reform" (Gong et al., 2016).

Xi has repeatedly emphasized the need to be aware of overcoming the "Thucydides Trap" and the "middle-income trap". The former is a political challenge, involving the management of relations with major countries like the United States. The latter is an economic issue, focusing on improving the quality and efficiency of China's economic development (Xi, 2017, p. 239).

Since the reform and opening-up, China's various capacities have grown explosively. Much of this capacity was formed during the golden period of global economic growth, aimed at external demand and the phase of rapid domestic growth. To counter the impact of the international financial crisis, some capacities were further expanded (Xi, 2017, p. 239).

Xi believes, given that the current problems are not cyclical, a short-term stimulus is unlikely to achieve a V-shaped rebound, and China's economy may experience an L-shaped growth stage. China needs to prepare for a prolonged struggle, dare to endure painful hardships, appropriately increase tolerance for downshifting and slowing down, first stabilizing the base and then rising. Xi (2017, p. 239) further suggests that China should face difficulties head-on, clarify direction, firm up confidence, work together, strengthen systemic dynamics and endogenous vitality, convert China's immense economic growth potential into reality, and lead China's economy to a new level.

Xi (2017, p. 245) concludes his remarks on the "new normal" with a historical and philosophical perspective: "From the perspective of the long historical process, new states, new patterns, and new stages in China's economic development are constantly emerging. The new normal of economic development is a phase in this long process. This fully conforms to the law of spiral upward development of things. To fully understand and grasp the new normal, we need to examine China's development from a broad perspective in both time and space".

Against this backdrop, the BRI emerged during the B Phase of the Kondratieff Cycle and aligns with China's L-Shaped growth trend. Thus, the purpose of the BRI was to foster China's continued opening-up and to help spur global economic development. In many respects, the BRI serves as a countercyclical tool for both China's and the global economy.

In summary, Xi Jinping's economic statecraft has been primarily focused on development, as he inherited a decelerating economy, despite its massive size. Fully aware of the impending challenges, Xi's initiatives, most notably the BRI, were primarily employed to spur economic development rather than to showcase China's prestige. As he himself emphasized that "the basic national condition that our country is still in and will be in the primary stage of socialism for a long time has not changed, and our country's international status as the world's largest developing country has not changed (Xi, 2017, p. 10)".

4.1.2 Xi Jinping's Marxist Approach to Economic Statecraft

Xi Jinping has shown some signs of approaching to a new economic statecraft in which Marxist ideology is given greater prominence to bolster the power of the ruling Communist Party at home and economic liberalism is de-emphasized in favor of an overarching framework of renaissance, aimed at a return to the status quo of pre-1840s colonial and post-colonial western domination (Zhang and Keith, 2017).

Xi Jinping's economic statecraft is heavily influenced by his worldview of Communist ideals. However, Xi's Communist ideals are not about spreading Communism across the world. Instead, he focuses on the long-term rule of the CPC within China. Xi Jinping's foreign policy thought, and theory system have clear goals, guiding China's diplomacy to achieve the great rejuvenation of the Chinese nation and promote peaceful development in the international community, advancing along the path of socialism with Chinese characteristics toward the direction of communism.

Domestically, Xi Jinping attaches great importance to and often emphasizes the education of ideals and beliefs of communists: "We must adhere to Marxism, firmly establish the lofty ideal of communism and the common ideal of socialism with Chinese characteristics (Xi, 2020, p. 18)". "(We must) deeply understand that achieving communism is a historical process achieved step by step through stage-by-stage goals, combining the lofty ideal of communism with the common ideal of socialism with Chinese characteristics and with the work we are currently doing(Xi, 2018)". "Communism is a long-term goal, and socialism is the first stage of communism(Xi, 2015)".

Internationally, Xi Jinping combines the communist ideal with the cause of human progress, stating: "The Communist Party of China is a party that seeks happiness for the Chinese people and also a party that struggles for the cause of human progress (Xi, 2020, p. 45)". To this end, he calls for the promotion of a new type of international relations and the construction of a community with a shared future for mankind. Based on reality, the current world, especially major countries, needs to build a new type of international relations based on mutual respect, fairness, justice, and win-win cooperation, and then strive to construct a community with a shared future for mankind. After the 18th National Congress of the CPC, Xi Jinping progressively advocated the communities of shared interests, responsibilities, and destiny. "Building a community with a shared future for mankind" was also included in the General Principles section of the Constitution of the CPC and the Preamble of the Constitution of the People's Republic of China (Yang, 2021).

Xi Jinping's "community of shared future" (often referred to as "community of shared destiny" in earlier translations) is a concept aimed at fostering a new type of international relations characterized by mutual respect, equity, justice, and win-win cooperation. It envisions a world where nations collaborate closely to address global challenges, promote peace, development, and shared prosperity, transcending differences in culture, political systems, and development stages.

Introduced by Chinese President Xi Jinping in 2013, this concept has become a cornerstone of China's foreign policy and its approach to global governance. It suggests that in an interconnected world, countries' destinies are intertwined, and they should work together to tackle issues like climate change, economic disparity, and security threats.

The community of shared future emphasizes:

- Global Governance: Advocating for a more equitable and fair international governance system.
- Sustainable Development: Promoting sustainable development practices worldwide.
- Cultural Exchange: Encouraging respect for diverse cultures and civilizations.
- Security Cooperation: Enhancing global security through cooperative initiatives.
- Economic Integration: Supporting open economies and opposing protectionism to achieve mutual economic growth.

This concept has been referenced in various international forums and incorporated into United Nations resolutions, reflecting China's ambition to play a more prominent role in global affairs, promoting a vision of globalization that is open, inclusive, balanced, and beneficial for all.

Xi Jinping's economic statecraft also has a Marxist internationalist flavor. China supports and assists developing countries, especially the least developed ones, in reducing poverty, improving people's livelihoods, and enhancing their development environments. China also urges developed countries to update their ideas and take action on development issues. For Chinese policy thinkers, the continuous development of the path, theory, system, and culture of socialism with Chinese characteristics has expanded the pathways for developing countries toward modernization. It provides a novel choice for countries and nations wishing to accelerate development while maintaining their independence, contributing Chinese wisdom and solutions to solving global human problems (Xi, 2020, pp. 8–9).

4.1.3 Xi Jinping's Historical Approach to Economic Statecraft Based on Confucius-Mencius Philosophy

Xi Jinping, like Mao Zedong before him, is a president deeply rooted in history. His governance and statecraft philosophy are significantly influenced by China's historical experiences and the Confucius-Mencius philosophy.

Xi Jinping is passionate about blending the promotion of excellent traditional culture with Marxist perspectives. He visited the Confucius Mansion and Temple in Shandong Province and made a special trip to the Zhu Xi Garden in Wuyi Mountain. During this latter visit, he stated, "We are committed to advancing socialism with Chinese characteristics and must promote the sinicization of Marxism. Without the 5,000-year-old Chinese civilization, where would the unique characteristics of China come from? Without these Chinese characteristics, how could we have such a successful path of socialism with Chinese characteristics today? It is crucial to place great importance on extracting the essence of the 5,000-year Chinese civilization, combining the promotion of excellent traditional culture with Marxist perspectives and methodologies, and steadfastly continue on the path of socialism with Chinese characteristics (The Communist Party, 2021)".

Xi's historical approach is manifested in the following aspects:

First, in the context of international relations, Xi Jinping views the preservation of sovereignty as his top priority. For all Chinese leaders since 1949, the memory of the Opium War and the subsequent century of humiliation has remained the most significant moral driving force behind national rejuvenation. The theory of Chinese diplomacy has always prioritized maintaining and developing national sovereignty.

That is why China is very tough when it comes to sovereignty issues. Since the 18th National Congress of the CPC, Xi has insisted on maintaining national sovereignty and territorial integrity in issues related to Taiwan, Hong Kong, and Xinjiang, taking decisive measures to protect national core interests. Xi (2018, p. 249) emphasizes: "We should never give up our legitimate rights and interests, nor should we sacrifice national core interests. No foreign country should expect us to trade our core interests or accept the bitter fruit that undermines our sovereignty, security, and development interests".

Second, Xi Jinping's Confucius-Mencius economic statecraft is evident in his proposal of what he calls "The Correct Concept of Righteousness and Interest". Xi Jinping emphasizes a value system in international relations that advocates morality, upholds justice, champions fairness, extends righteousness, prioritizes righteousness over interest, and places interest after righteousness.

The traditional Chinese philosophy of righteousness and interest advocates "A gentleman values righteousness as his substance", emphasizing "A nation does not take interest as profit, but righteousness as profit", and believes that "Wealth and honor unrighteously acquired are to me as floating clouds". In short, the traditional Chinese culture's concept of righteousness and interest highlights righteousness, stressing the importance of righteousness over interest. This has also become a consistent moral norm and behavioral guideline for China's foreign relations.

Xi Jinping combines Marxism with traditional Confucius-Mencius philosophy by proposing the socialist concept of righteousness and interest. Xi Jinping pointed out: "Righteousness reflects our concept, the concept of Communists and socialist countries (Wang, 2013d)". The correct concept of righteousness and interest emphasizes the "righteousness" of global justice and the "interest" shared by humanity, completely conforming to China's national positioning as a major global, socialist, and developing country.

In practice, China has highlighted "righteousness" while also taking care of "interest", achieving a balance and consideration of both righteousness and interest under the precedence of "righteousness", thus realizing both gains in righteousness and interest.

In conclusion, Xi Jinping began implementing what he termed "Major-Country Diplomacy" during his first term. The core of this diplomatic approach was to convert China's economic strengths into international influence and power, aiming to fulfill Xi's Marxist ideals and reestablish China's historic central role on the global stage. However, Xi's ambitions were tempered by China's economic slowdown, necessitating a continuation of the traditional developmentalist approach initiated during Deng Xiaoping's era.

4.2 Xi Jinping's Major-Country Diplomacy with Chinese Characteristics (2017–2022)

In comparison to Hu Jintao, Xi Jinping appears much more at ease on the international stage. His approach to diplomacy has been significantly more active than Hu's.

However, when Xi came to power, he encountered an increasingly challenging diplomatic landscape, marked by the dilemma of balancing China's rise with a complex and evolving international environment. On one hand, China's growing strength and resources enabled it to cultivate a more favorable international environment. On the other hand, it confronted an increasingly challenging, at times even hostile, global context. At this juncture, Chinese diplomacy was at a crossroads, in dire need of a significant breakthrough.

To make a diplomatic breakthrough, Xi Jinping pressed for a new type of diplomacy, which his Foreign Minister Wang Yi (2013a) labeled as "Major-Country Diplomacy with Chinese characteristics".

There are clear rationales and objectives behind Xi's distinctive approach to major-country diplomacy, deeply rooted in the guiding principles of the CPC and Xi Jinping's ideological framework:

1 Upholding the CPC's Founding Mission: It emphasizes that for over a century, the CPC has aimed to make significant contributions to humanity, distinguishing its approach to diplomacy from traditional Western practices. This approach is underpinned by the core values of socialism with Chinese characteristics, a commitment to defending the socialist path chosen by the Chinese people, and a dedication to promoting world peace, common development, and building a community with a shared future for mankind.
2 Achieving National Rejuvenation: Since the 18th CPC National Congress, China's comprehensive national power and international status have significantly increased, moving the nation closer to the center stage of the world and the goal of great national rejuvenation. In this journey, China faces both strategic opportunities and challenges, with uncertainties and risks in the changing international system. Therefore, a major-country diplomacy with Chinese characteristics is deemed necessary to foster a peaceful and stable international and regional environment, essential for achieving national rejuvenation.
3 Responding to Global Changes: The world is undergoing profound shifts in the balance of international forces and global structure, characterized by multipolarity, economic globalization, and democratization of international relations. However, challenges like unilateralism, protectionism, and hegemonism persist, leading to a new period of turbulence and transformation. Xi Jinping emphasizes the importance of China's role in offering its voice and solutions to the international community. As a major country with a rich 5,000-year civilization and a permanent member of the UN Security Council, China sees it as necessary to engage in major-country diplomacy with its own characteristics, fulfilling its international responsibilities and obligations. This approach aims to forge a new path of peaceful development and win-win cooperation, promote common values of humanity, and jointly build a community with a shared future for mankind (Wang, 2022).

4.2.1 A Case Study: Xi Jinping's Approach to the US

Guided by Communist principles and driven by a strong desire for national rejuvenation, Xi Jinping started his diplomatic revolution characterized by his personal style, confidence, ideals, and ambition. The first thing is to get the US-China relations right.

During his meeting with Obama at the Annenberg Retreat in Sunnylands, California, in 2013, Xi Jinping and Obama agreed to establish a new type of major-country relationship. Xi Jinping believed that the essential question facing US-China relations is whether and how to overcome the so-called "Thucydides Trap", the inevitable confrontation between a rising power and an established one. The new type of major-country relationship fit well with Xi Jinping's major-country diplomatic vision and helped to maintain the overall stability of the US-China relationship during Xi's first term.

As a matter of fact, as early as in February 2012, the then Vice President Xi Jinping, during his visit to the United States, had already proposed that China and the United States should embark on a new path of major-country relations. In March 2012, during the fourth round of the China-US Strategic and Economic Dialogue, the Chinese side focused on explaining its policy concepts and comprehensive propositions for constructing a new model of major-country relations between China and the United States (Dai, 2016, p. 172). Dai Bingguo, the former State Councilor in charge of foreign relations under Hu Jintao's leadership, stated in his memoire that, in fact, "new model of major-country relations" is not a new term; since the first round of the China-US Strategic Dialogue (in 2009), both sides have been progressively exploring in-depth how to avoid conflict and confrontation, and jointly work toward developing a new model of major-country relations characterized by mutual respect and win-win cooperation (Dai, 2016, pp. 172–173).

The consensus between Obama and Xi on developing a new model of major-country relationship was significant for Xi's first term, as it largely stabilized China's external relationships. This consensus also represents a continuation of the strategic management of great power relations that began in 2006 with the establishment of the Strategic Economic Dialogue between the United States and China.

However, the Obama-Xi consensus signifies different things to Obama and Xi. For Obama, it implies that China's rise will be framed within an institutional framework led by the United States. For Xi, it means that China will continue to ascend with a fully-fledged new diplomatic agenda, one that is destined to change the world and restore China to its rightful historical central position.

On May 21, 2014, in Shanghai, Xi Jinping's major-country diplomacy took the world by surprise. At the Conference on Interaction and Confidence Building Measures in Asia (CICA), China introduced a diplomatic concept known as the "Asian Security Concept". This was quickly criticized and likened to a "Chinese version of the Monroe Doctrine" (The Paper, 2014). What Xi Jinping specifically stated was, "Ultimately, the affairs of Asia must be managed by the people of Asia; the problems of Asia must be resolved by the people of Asia; the security of Asia must be upheld by the people of Asia. The people of Asia have the capability and wisdom to achieve peace and stability in Asia through strengthened cooperation (Xinhuanet, 2014)".

The core of this new Asian Security Concept is to promote the idea that "Asian countries should lead Asian affairs", aiming to emphasize China's leadership role in the Asia-Pacific region. This move is seen by the international community as China's attempt to reshape the regional security architecture and its comprehensive competition with the United States in the Asia-Pacific. Particularly during the preparation of the CICA, the changes in China's diplomatic discourse attracted attention from Western countries and neighboring countries of China.

That is why we argue that Xi Jinping's new diplomatic approach represents not merely a readjustment but a diplomatic revolution. His diplomacy is rooted in Marxism and is driven by the historical ambition of restoring China to its rightful central position in history. According to Xi Jinping, the biggest challenge China faces is still the suppression by a coalition of Western countries led by the US hegemon. The dominance of Western institutions at a global level has become a barrier to the development of emerging developing nations. This is a long-term problem that cannot be quickly resolved. To overcome these challenges of rising and development, China needs to make concerted efforts at the global level and within the international system, aiming to achieve new forms of development (Wang, 2022).

4.3 Xi Jinping's Governance Revolution

While Jiang Zemin and Hu Jintao are regarded as continuations of Deng Xiaoping's policies, Xi Jinping represents a departure in many aspects. Indeed, Xi's approach can be seen as a revival of Mao Zedong's principles. However, Xi's resemblance to Mao was not very evident during his first term. It was only during his second and third terms that these similarities gradually became more pronounced.

That being said, traces of Xi's similarities to Mao can still be observed by comparing his leadership style and policies with those of Hu Jintao:

1 Emphasis on Political Philosophy and Ideology: Xi Jinping emphasizes the importance of Socialism with Chinese characteristics and the Chinese Dream, as well as the goal of the great rejuvenation of the Chinese nation. During Hu Jintao's tenure, there was more emphasis on building a "harmonious society".
2 Anti-Corruption Campaign: After coming to power, Xi Jinping initiated an unprecedented anti-corruption campaign to purify the Party and government, with the goal of enhancing government efficiency and credibility. In contrast, Hu Jintao did not launch an anti-corruption campaign on the same scale as Xi's.
3 Centralization of Power: Xi Jinping strengthened centralization, enhancing the power and influence of central leadership. In contrast, during

Hu Jintao's era, the distribution of power between the central and local governments was more balanced.

4 Economic Reforms: Xi Jinping has championed supply-side structural reforms, placing an emphasis on innovation-driven and high-quality development. In contrast, Hu Jintao's tenure was characterized by a focus on stable growth and expanding domestic demand. During Xi's first term, there was a notable embrace of reform and opening-up policies, which had undertones of economic liberalism. This stance becomes particularly notable considering Xi's pivot away from economic liberalism toward the end of his second term and into his third.
5 Military Reforms: Xi Jinping undertook profound military reforms, including restructuring military regions and promoting the integration of military and civilian development.
6 Establishment of the National Supervisory Law and the National Supervision Commission: During Xi Jinping's tenure, China passed the National Supervisory Law and established the National Supervision Commission, further strengthening anti-corruption and government oversight mechanisms.
7 Ideological Control: During Xi Jinping's tenure, there was increased control over ideology, emphasizing the importance of the Party's leadership and social stability. On November 17, 2012, shortly after being elected as the General Secretary of the CPC, Xi Jinping, while presiding over the first group study session of the 18th Central Politburo, made explicit demands for upholding the Party's leadership. He emphasized that "in all aspects of party, government, military, civilian, and academia, and across all regions – east, west, south, north, and center, the Party is the leader of everything (People, 2022)".

These changes reflect Xi Jinping's different views and strategies on China's future development and global status and also highlight the differences in focus and methods in governance and statecraft compared to Hu Jintao.

Notes

1 "The Silk Road Economic Belt", "The 21st Century Maritime Silk Road", "China-India-Myanmar-Bangladesh Economic Corridor", "China-Pakistan Economic Corridor", "Asian Infrastructure Investment Bank", and "BRICS Development Bank".
2 The concept of "High-Speed Rail Diplomacy" was first proposed by Hong Kong's "South China Morning Post" in an article titled "China Plans to Build a Trans-Eurasian Railway Network" published on March 8, 2010. The article posited that negotiations were underway regarding China's plans to expand its high-speed rail network to 17 countries. These railways would connect and open up the whole of Central Asia, East Asia, and Southeast Asia, aiding China in more efficiently transporting vital raw materials. Targeting neighboring countries such as those in Southeast Asia and Central Asia as markets for its high-speed railways has become an important aspect of China's foreign policy. Through "High-Speed Rail Diplomacy",

China is actively constructing a high-speed rail network originating within its borders to facilitate the import of energy resources like coal and iron ore and expand its influence in neighboring countries.

3 China's "Nuclear Power Diplomacy" began in the 1980s, when it introduced technology and capital from France, a nuclear power powerhouse, to start building the Daya Bay Nuclear Power Plant in Guangdong. Starting from Daya Bay, Sino-French nuclear cooperation has gone through three stages: initially "French-led with Chinese assistance", then transitioning to "Chinese-led with French support", and finally to "joint design and construction". China's nuclear technology capabilities have continuously grown stronger. In recent years, it has started to participate in international competition. A significant breakthrough was made in 2013 in its "going global" strategy when China National Nuclear Corporation and China General Nuclear Power Group, in collaboration with two French companies, reached an agreement with the British government to build two third-generation pressurized water reactor nuclear units at Hinkley Point in the southwest of England. This marked the first time Chinese nuclear technology entered a developed country. After Xi Jinping and the new leadership took office, Chinese national leaders have increasingly used nuclear power as a diplomatic card during their visits abroad, promoting cooperation in the field of nuclear power between both sides.

Reference List

CGTN (2019) *Xi says Belt and Road Initiative Is Not China's Marshall Plan.* [online] Available at: https://news.cgtn.com/news/3d3d514e3559544d35457a6333566d54/index.html.

Dai, B. G. (2016) *Strategic Dialogue: Memoirs of Dai Bingguo.* Beijing: People's Publishing House.

Gong, W., Xu, Z. F., and Wang, K. (2016) *Authoritative People on China's Contemporary Economy: The Supply-Side Reform Guides the New Normal* [People's Daily] 4 January. Available at: http://politics.people.com.cn/n1/2016/0104/c1001-28006547.html.

Gong, W., Xu, Z. F., and Wu, Q. Y. (2016) *Authoritative People Talking about China's Economy* [People's Daily] 9 May. Available at: http://politics.people.com.cn/n1/2016/0509/c1001-28333725.html.

People (2014) *Xi Jinping Emphasized during His Visit to Henan Province: Deepening Reforms and Giving Full Play to Advantages, Innovating Ideas and Taking a Balanced Approach to Ensure Sustained and Healthy Economic Development and Social Harmony and Stability* [People] 11 May. Available at: http://cpc.people.com.cn/n/2014/0511/c64094-25001070.html.

People (2022) *The Party, the Government, the Military, the People, the East, the West, the South, the North, the South, the South, the North, the Party Is the Leader of All* [People] 14 February. Available at: http://dangjian.people.com.cn/n1/2022/0214/c117092-32351226.html.

Publicity Department of the Communist Party of China (2016) *Xi Jinping General Secretary Series of Important Lectures Readings.* Beijing: Xue Xi Chu Ban She.

The Communist Party (2021) *The Governance of China IV: Combining the Promotion of Outstanding Traditional Culture with Marxist Position and Viewpoint Methods* [The Communist Party] 22 March. Available at: https://www.12371.cn/2022/09/21/ARTI1663740589405824.shtml.

The Paper (2014) *Looking at ASIM: The False Perception of 'China's Version of the Monroe Doctrine'* [The Paper] 24 June. Available at: https://www.thepaper.cn/newsDetail_forward_1246742.

Wang, F. (2017) "The Origin, Achievements, and Development of China's Diplomacy as a Major Power with Chinese Characteristics", *World Affairs*. (07), p. 10.

Wang, F. (2022) "Great Power Diplomacy with Chinese Characteristics: Huge Change in Situation and Enhancement of Historical Mission", *Pacific Journal*. 30(06), pp. 1–15.

Wang, Y. (2013d) *Adhering to the Correct Concept of Righteousness and Benefit, and Actively Playing the Role of a Responsible Great Power* [People] 10 September. Available at: http://opinion.people.com.cn/n/2013/0910/c1003-22862978.html.

Wang, Y. (2013a) *Exploring the Path of Major-Country Diplomacy with Chinese Characteristics*. At the Luncheon of the Second World Peace Forum, 27 June. Available at: https://www.mfa.gov.cn/eng/wjb_663304/wjbz_663308/2461_663310/201306/t20130627_468425.html.

Wang, Y. (2022) *Comprehensively Promoting China's Diplomacy as a Major Country with Chinese Characteristics* [People Daily] 8 November.

Wang, Y. (2022) *Comprehensively Promoting Great-Country Diplomacy with Chinese Characteristics* [People's Daily] 8 November. Available at: https://paper.people.com.cn/rmrb/html/2022-11/08/nw.D110000renmrb_20221108_1-06.htm.

Xi, J. P. (2017) *The Governance of China. II*. Beijing, China: Foreign Languages Press.

Xi, J. P. (2018) *The Governance of China*. Beijing, China: Foreign Languages Press.

Xi, J. P. (2020) *The Governance of China. III*. Beijing, China: Foreign Languages Press.

Xinhuanet (2014) *Address by Mr. Jinping at the Fourth Summit of the Conference on Interaction and Confidence-Building Measures in Asia (CICA)* [Xinhuanet] 21 May. Available at: http://www.xinhuanet.com/world/2014-05/21/c_1110796357.htm.

Yang, J. M. (2021) "Exploring the Theoretical System of Xi Jinping's Diplomatic Thought." *International Studies*. (02), pp. 1–19.

Zhang, X. T., and Keith, J.. (2017) "From Wealth to Power: China's New Economic Statecraft", *The Washington Quarterly*. 40(1), pp. 185–203. doi: 10.1080/0163660X.2017.1302746.

Zhong, S. (2017) "Achieving New Development, New Improvement and New Breakthroughs in Commercial Business – In-Depth Study of General Secretary Xi Jinping's Important Thoughts on Economic Diplomacy", *Qiushi*. (18), pp. 22–24.

5 Xi Jinping's Economic Statecraft in the Era of Dramatic Changes Unseen in a Century (2018–2023)

The year 2018 was a watershed moment, marking the beginning of Xi Jinping's challenging second term. In many ways, 2018 represented a climax after several years of upheaval both domestically and on the global stage. Domestically, 2014 marked a transitional year as China's economy began to slowdown, leading Xi Jinping to introduce the concept of the "Economic New Normal". In 2016, the strains in China's economy became even more apparent. The pandemic, which started in Wuhan in December 2019, further devastated China's economy. On the global front, we witnessed significant events including the Russia-Ukraine crisis, Brexit, and the election of Donald Trump as the US President, a populist leader who caused a major, unexpected shock in global diplomacy. Trump's transactional approach to diplomacy and his bullying style took many world leaders by surprise.

Xi Jinping was likely the first global leader to perceive the significant changes of our times, and he has a strong sense of urgency. As early as 2017, he recognized that we were experiencing profound shifts not seen in a century ("百年未有之大变局") (Xi, 2018). President Xi Jinping proposed this concept at the 2017 annual conference for Chinese ambassadors and consuls abroad: "Socialism with Chinese characteristics has entered a new era. To do a good job in diplomatic work in the new era, we must first deeply understand the spirit of the 19th National Congress of the Communist Party of China and correctly grasp the current trends of the times and the international situation. Looking at the world, we are facing a great change not seen in a century (Xinhuanet, 2017)".

Six months later, Xi further elaborated on this concept by distinguishing between the domestic and global situations: "Currently, our country is in the best development period since modern times, and the world is undergoing a great change not seen in a century. The two are intertwined and interact with each other (Xinhuanet, 2018)".

When he first proposed this concept, many were skeptical, questioning whether we were indeed on the brink of dramatic changes akin to those last witnessed during the First World War. Gradually, as numerous "gray rhino" and "black swan" events unfolded one after another, people became convinced.

DOI: 10.4324/9781003270379-6

Recognizing the shifting tides doesn't necessarily mean that China was fully prepared or managed all crises effectively. While it's challenging to make generalizations, it's fair to say that China's relationship with Western countries deteriorated, whereas its relations with developing nations generally improved. This dynamic also signals a new form of Cold War, with China and the United States leading two not entirely defined camps.

During Xi Jinping's second term (2017–2022), China's economic statecraft faced considerable challenges as the country's economy slowed significantly and its relationship with the West deteriorated. Despite these difficulties, China demonstrated notable resilience during and after the pandemic.

5.1 China's Diplomatic Confrontation with the West

Since Xi Jinping assumed office, China's diplomatic elites have increasingly embraced the belief of "The East Rises and the West Declines" (东升西降) (People, 2021). The concept of "East Rising, West Declining" was articulated by Xi Jinping on various occasions since 2021. During the pandemic, Xi Jinping (2022) also articulated the concept of "Good Governance in China and Chaos in the West" (中治西乱). These statements reflect the worsening US-China relationship and Xi Jinping's efforts to bolster national confidence in China. This concept bears a striking resemblance to Mao Zedong's assertion in November 1957 about the "East Wind prevailing over the West Wind".

We must bear in mind that there is a distinctive shift in Xi Jinping's attitude toward the United States. When he met Obama in 2013, the US-China relationship was still in good shape, and it was highly unlikely that Xi would publicly articulate concepts like "East Rising, West Declining" or "Good Governance in China and Western Chaos". For many years before Xi, China's diplomatic narrative largely accepted America's leadership, with the United States in turn welcoming China's peaceful rise. Therefore, to understand Xi's attitude shift, it is necessary to identify the factors and timeline of the deterioration in the US-China relationship.

The year 2018 was a turning point for US-China relations. Before Trump's rise to power and its aggressive unilateral stance on trade, the Chinese reacted to Americans increased presence in their neighborhood by the adoption of a strategy characterized by summit and economic diplomacy, an effort to stabilize China-US economic and trade relations. In hope of pursuing on the same diplomatic path, on April 6–7, 2017, within 100 days of President Trump's accession to the White House, Chinese President Xi Jinping met with the latter at Mar-a-Lago in Florida, claiming that "there are a thousand reasons to make the China-US relationship work, and no reason to break it"(People's Daily, 2017). China and the United States have also agreed *on a Comprehensive Economic Dialogue*, the first of which was held in Washington on July 19, 2017. On the surface, everything seemed to run smoothly during the first visit to China by President Trump on 8th–10th November of the same year.

China agreed to a major purchase of American goods, amounting to US$253.5 billion, including a Chinese pledge to buy 300 aircraft from Boeing, with a list value of $38 billion. The Chinese also agreed to import up to $12 billion in mobile phone chips and made a commitment to invest $83 billion in the US petrochemical industry to develop shale gases. The agreement did not assuage Trump's aggressive stance, as he judged that the Chinese proposal would do little to redress his country's commercial imbalance toward Beijing. As negotiations were ongoing, Americans maintained the pressure. In fact, as early as August 18, 2017, one month after the conclusion of the *Comprehensive Economic Dialogue* and three months before Trump's visit to China, the American president signed the *Presidential Memorandum on the Actions by the United States Related to the Section 301 Investigation* to probe whether Chinese laws and regulations implement mandatory technology transfer and whether it harms US intellectual property and innovation. This shows that President Trump was maintaining a double-edged trading strategy, as he planned to launch a "trade offensive" against China, even before his visit to China. It soon became clear that Trump would pursue a strategy of aggressive unilateralism over negotiations with his Chinese counterpart.

On December 18, 2017, just one month after his visit to China, Trump's administration unveiled its first *National Security Strategy Report*, which identified China as a "competitor", "rival", and "adversary". This formulation was far more stringent than any reports put forth by previous administrations. Harsh words led to quick actions. On March 22, 2018, the Trump administration announced on the basis of its 301 investigation that punitive tariffs will be slapped on some US$50 billion worth of imports from China due to intellectual property infringement. China immediately counterattacked, marking the outbreak of the China-US trade war. From that point on, the trade war has escalated with nearly all Chinese exports to the United States covered by punitive tariffs, and the United States has even considered the "decoupling" of Chinese and American economies as a potential policy option (New York Times, 2019).

The launch of the trade war against China by President Trump triggered a far-reaching ideological competition between China and the United States, the two leading countries in the world, effectively plunging the world into a new Cold War. As Susan Shirk suggested, Xi Jinping also casted the relationship with the West as a cold-war-type ideological contest between socialism and capitalism. Socialism with Chinese characteristics would triumph over capitalism and have increasingly greater influence in the world. Officials in both the Trump and Biden administrations framed the relationship as a contest between the two systems, Chinese communist autocracy versus Western market democracy (Shirk, 2023, p. 184).

Against this backdrop, China's diplomatic approach has increasingly shifted toward "Wolf Warrior Diplomacy" (战狼外交). The term "Wolf Warrior Diplomacy" reflects a more assertive trend in China's foreign policy in recent years. This term originates from the 2015 movie "Wolf Warrior", directed by Wu Jing, which showcased strong nationalist sentiments. The film, gaining widespread attention, told the legendary story of an underdog hero rising to save his country's and nation's fate. The term began to gain attention on December 8, 2020, when Germany's Der Spiegel published a report criticizing China's foreign policy. The report described Chinese diplomats' behavior as "more aggressive" and pointed out that China had adopted "Wolf Warrior Diplomacy". The core characteristic of "Wolf Warrior Diplomacy" is its toughness and directness. This diplomatic style is seen as a label for China's assertive foreign policy since Xi Jinping became General Secretary of the Communist Party of China. Western countries believe that during this period, Chinese diplomats and leaders have shown a provocative attitude, issuing a series of aggressive statements. The underlying policy of this diplomatic strategy dates back to the 18th National Congress of the Communist Party of China in 2012, when Xi Jinping ascended to power and promoted the policy of "advancing major-country diplomacy with Chinese characteristics, with the mission of achieving the great rejuvenation of the Chinese nation". A key concept of this policy is "daring to show the sword", meaning to adopt a tough stance at critical moments. In the international community, "Wolf Warrior Diplomacy" has become one of China's diplomatic brands. For example, China's most senior foreign policy official, Yang Jiechi, has told the United States that it isn't qualified to "speak from a position of strength" when criticizing China (BBC, 2021). It is also seen as an embodiment of "Wolf Warrior Diplomacy".

5.2 China's Strained Economy

China's economy slowed down from a double-digit pace in the decade up to 2011 to a range of 6–7% since then. Notably, the economy began to slowdown significantly in 2018. China's GDP growth rate decreased from 7.9% in 2012 to 6.7% in 2018 (World Bank, 2023). In 2015, Xi Jinping (2017, p. 239) persuaded the Chinese people that this was the "New Normal". He stated that since the current problem is mainly structural rather than cyclical, a V-shaped rebound through short-term stimulation was impossible, and China's economy may experience an L-shaped growth phase. Xi warned of the need to be prepared for a protracted battle, to be willing to endure significant challenges, to appropriately increase tolerance for gear shifting and slowing down, to first establish a foundation, and then aim for recovery. Xi's policy solution in 2015 was supply-side structural reform, a policy also associated with Premier Li Keqiang.

The concept of supply-side economics emerged in the 1970s as a response to stagflation (simultaneous inflation and stagnant economic growth), challenging the then-dominant Keynesian emphasis on demand management. Supply-side reforms gained prominence in the United States during the

Reagan administration in the 1980s, which argued that reducing taxes and regulatory burdens would lead to increased production, job creation, and economic growth.

In the context of China, supply-side structural reform became a significant policy focus under the leadership of Xi Jinping. The Chinese government officially endorsed the concept at the Central Economic Work Conference in December 2015 (People, 2015). The reforms were introduced to address various structural imbalances in the Chinese economy, such as overcapacity in certain industries (like steel and coal), real estate bubbles, and the need for a transition from an investment-driven to a more consumption- and innovation-driven growth model. The primary objectives of China's supply-side structural reforms include: deleveraging (reducing the high levels of debt within the economy, particularly corporate debt), reducing overcapacity, destocking (reducing high levels of unsold real estate inventory), improving corporate efficiency, and risk mitigation (addressing financial risks and ensuring stability in the financial sector).

China's economy slowed further during Xi Jinping's second term (2017–2022), with the annual growth rate decreasing from 6.7% in 2018 to 2.2% in 2020. This considerable economic slowdown since 2018 is attributed more to policy management and exogenous shocks than to a natural economic slowdown trajectory, a situation Xi Jinping has originally referred to as the "New Normal". Key contributing factors include the US-China trade war in 2018 that continued until January 2020, and the COVID-19, which further devastated China's economy. People began questioning why the economy slid so drastically and why social stresses were increasing.

The West started to feel China's economic slowdown during and after the COVID-19 and heavily criticized Xi Jinping for deviating from market principles. Nicholas Lardy (2019, p. 4), a senior researcher of Peterson Institute, argues, one of the most important contributors to China's slowing economic growth is the slowing pace of domestic economic reform and the resurgence of the role of the state in resource allocation. These trends stifled the competitive forces that had previously powered the Chinese economy, placing more investment in poorly performing and indeed deteriorating state-owned enterprises. Nicholas Lardy's analysis shows that a main driving factor was the turn away from the market orientation that guided economic reform for more than three decades starting in 1978. But a visible change in strategy, in favor of state-led growth, accelerated under the leadership of Xi Jinping starting in 2012 (Posen, 2019, p. x).

It remains debatable whether Xi Jinping has abandoned market principles. If he has, it is puzzling why he underwent a U-turn in his attitude toward the market. Back in November 2013, at the Third Plenary Session of the 18th Central Committee of the Communist Party of China, President Xi Jinping particularly emphasized the market's decisive role in resource allocation. This stance left the world with the impression that Xi would continue to advance the market economy. Additionally, in 2013–2014, China commenced investment liberalization negotiations with both the United States and the EU through the framework of a Bilateral Investment Treaty (BIT). Concurrently, trade liberalization talks were initiated within the Regional Comprehensive Economic Partnership Agreement (RCEP). Shanghai was established as China's first Free Trade Zone (FTZ), where investment liberalization was trialed in preparation for the US-China BIT negotiations. This led many to believe that a new era of China's reform and opening-up was on the horizon.

To be fair, throughout Xi Jinping's first term, he, along with Li Keqiang, the Chinese Premier, and other Chinese leaders, consistently pursued pro-market and pro-opening up measures. A notable outcome of these efforts was the conclusion of the RCEP negotiations in 2020. Additionally, FTZ pilot areas have been established across China, showcasing the tangible progress of these initiatives. However, negotiations with the United States on the BIT were suspended after Trump assumed power, and the EU-China BIT failed to be ratified following the EU's imposition of human rights sanctions on China that related to China's human rights violations in Xinjiang. In response, China retaliated by sanctioning the European Parliament and the Political and Security Committee of the Council of Ministers of the EU. Consequently, China's economic liberalization initiatives faced significant challenges as its relationships with both the United States and the EU reached a low point. Additionally, China's relations with Canada deteriorated after Ms. Wanzhou Meng was placed under house arrest in Canada.

The debate over whether and why Xi Jinping changed his attitude toward the market is complex. I argue that Xi does not intend to abandon his pro-market stance. In fact, he has never completely forsaken pro-market reforms and the policy of opening up. However, internal and external pressures have forced him to adopt more state intervention, often appearing to turn his back on the market. Xi increasingly believes that Western capitalist countries, led by the United States, aim to contain China, restrict its rise, and ultimately undermine its Communist regime. Faced with Trump's aggressive tactics in the trade war, Xi chose a tit-for-tat approach. In Trump's cabinet, Cold War hawks and ideologues viewed the US-China rivalry as inevitable, a duel between the just and the unjust, representing both ideological competition and a clash of systems. This external pressure has pushed Xi Jinping to rely more on friendly Belt and Road Initiative (BRI) countries, including Russia. Increasingly, China has begun to use economic sanctions against countries it believes have violated the "One China" policy, such as Lithuania, which allowed Taiwan to establish a representative office in the name of Taiwan instead of Chinese Taipei (Reynolds and Goodman, 2022).

Domestically, Xi Jinping's ideological pureness had some conflicts with part of China's private economy. Xi's ideological stance, deeply rooted in Marxism-Leninism, has evolved into a more pronounced framework since his earliest political writings in 2013, and particularly after the 19th Party

Congress in 2017. This ideological framework has increasingly intertwined with China's economic policy, leading to a nuanced and sometimes contentious relationship with the private sector. The 20th Party Congress report at the end of 2022 reflected a heavier ideological tone compared to the previous 40 years, emphasizing Marxism-Leninism as the fundamental ideological framework. This shift was also represented in the decreasing emphasis on economic development and a growing focus on national security in party documents. Xi also stepped up a simultaneous crackdown on internet entrepreneurs and the property and financial sectors, crucial economic drivers, that further slowed growth and scared away private and foreign investors (Leahy et al., 2023).

The COVID-19 dealt a further blow to China's already struggling economy. Xi Jinping's initial zero-COVID policy achieved success and increased his popularity and kept China's economy growing. However, the Shanghai lockdown from March to June 2022 was largely a policy failure, significantly damaging the economy of the Yangtze River Delta. This region, the economic heartland of China, includes Shanghai, Jiangsu Province, Zhejiang Province, and Anhui Province. The lockdown also caused widespread dissatisfaction among the Chinese people with Xi's pandemic policies. As a result, Xi Jinping ultimately decided to end China's zero-COVID policy in December 2022.

5.3 Xi's Economic Statecraft: Challenges, Retrenchment, and Resilience

The greatest challenge facing China's economic statecraft is balancing wealth growth with power projection. Xi Jinping's second term (2017–2022) witnessed a further slowdown in China's economy. Meanwhile, China's relationships with Western countries reached a low point, further straining China's economic growth. This is significant since Western countries are among China's most important trade and investment partners and major sources of capital and technology.

There was a significant shift in the approaches to economic statecraft between China and Western countries from Xi Jinping's first term to his second term. During Xi's first term, China and the West largely adopted strategies known as positive economic statecraft, including free trade and investment agreements, as well as summits. However, in the second term, the focus shifted toward negative economic statecraft strategies, such as economic warfare, which became more prevalent.

During Xi Jinping's first term, China, the United States, and the EU were actively engaged in negotiating investment treaties and managing their differences through strategic economic dialogues. The US-China Strategic and Economic Dialogue, established in 2009, remained operational during Xi's first term. Similarly, the EU-China High-Level Economic and Trade Dialogue (HED), ongoing since 2008, continued its function. Despite some challenges,

China's external environment was relatively stable and peaceful during this period. However, the situation shifted toward economic conflict in Xi Jinping's second term. The United States initiated a trade war against China in 2018, and the EU imposed human rights sanctions on China in 2020, leading to the suspension of the ratification process for the EU-China BIT. Furthermore, China's relationships with Canada, Japan, and Australia encountered significant difficulties, adversely affecting the smoothness of economic and trade relations.

A key global aspect of economic statecraft is the competition between the economic statecraft strategies of major powers. In other words, the economic statecraft of one great power often prompts reactive economic statecraft strategies from other great powers, leading to what can be likened to an "arms race" in the realm of economic statecraft. This phenomenon is referred to as "competing economic statecrafts" (Zhang, 2024).

China's launch of BRI in 2013 marks a watershed in the new age of competing economic statecraft. Its global coverage and large-scale leveraging of economic resources put China in the spotlight of global political economy. As a positive instrument of economic statecraft, the BRI spurred the United States to come up with competing connectivity projects, first the B3W initiative ("Build Back Better the World") announced by President Joe Biden in June 2021, and then the PGII (the Partnership for Global Infrastructure and Investment) announced in G7 Summit in June 2022, which intended to raise USD600 billion over the next five years to provide developing countries with financing for infrastructure development. Although China was not explicitly mentioned in the statement, the PGII was widely seen as an "alternative" to the BRI, aimed at weakening the international influence of the BRI. In May 2022, the Biden Administration established the Indo-Pacific Economic Framework (IPEF) with India, Australia, Japan, South Korea, and several ASEAN countries. A significant supply chain agreement under this framework was reached in November 2023. Since China's launch of BRI, the EU came up with a series of positive economic statecraft projects, including the EU Strategy for Cooperation in the Indo-Pacific, the EU-Asia Connectivity Strategy, the Globally Connected Europe Strategy, and the EU Global Gateway initiative in 2020–2022.

From a longer perspective, China's economic statecraft is a response to the US economic statecraft represented by the "New Silk Road Initiative" (US State Department Archived Content, 2009) and the "Asia Pivot" (Clinton, 2011) envisioned in 2011. The BRI is "China's March West" in response to Obama-Clinton's Asia Pivot (Wang, 2012). China's negotiation of RCEP was to respond to the US-led TPP. China's talks with the United States and the EU for BITs were to boost domestic reform and introduce the most advanced international economic rules so as to catch up with the highest level of economic rule-making. In summary, we are currently experiencing a phase of competing connectivity, where connectivity (and interdependence) is not only instrumentalized but also weaponized. In this "arms race" of competing connectivity strategies, China has been actively involved.

In the dark days of the world economy and warring states period of global economic statecraft, we are witnessing dramatic innovation of economic statecraft toolkits. To deny Russia the financial resources to fund its invasion of Ukraine, the US-led coalition immobilized Russia's sovereign wealth fund and central bank reserves (Adeyemo, 2022). To deny China's ability to acquire or develop high-end chips as well as reducing the dependence on critical technologies from China, the United States passed the Chips Act 2022 (The White House, 2022). To stand for its values, the EU established a global human rights sanctions regime on December 7, 2020, which allows it to target individuals, entities, and bodies – including state and non-state actors – responsible for, involved in or associated with serious human rights violations and abuses worldwide, no matter where they occurred (The Council of the EU, 2020). This global human rights sanctions regime has been applied on several occasions, including those against Russia and China. The EU's sanctions against China on the ground of human rights violations in Xinjiang triggered China's furious countersanctions.

The EU stands out in practicing trade statecraft since Von Der Leyen became President of the European Commission in 2019. At the EU level, a series of trade legislations have been proposed with geopolitical implications, such as Anti-Economic Coercion Instrument (ACI), aimed at countering the use of economic coercion by third countries (European Commission, 2021). The European Commission also proposed the Due Diligence Directive, International Procurement Instrument, and Anti-Subsidy Regulation, all of which are giving teeth to the EU to increase its capabilities in adapting to the birth of a "Geopolitical Europe" (European Council on Foreign Relations, 2022).

Apart from innovation of toolkit, the negotiation strategies of economic statecraft are also going through "smart" reconfiguration. As the world seems to enter a multipolar world, the global politics of economic statecraft seems to enter an era of strategic triangle among the United States, the EU, and China. The Biden's administration successfully revived the Atlantic alliance despite some trade disagreements. Russia's invasion of Ukraine largely reunited the West. President Von Der Leyen has emerged as the person to call when US officials want to call Europe (Lynch and Gridneff, 2022). The United States is aware that sanctions are most effective when coordinated with allies and partners, both because coordination bolsters diplomacy and because multilateral sanctions are harder to evade (Adeyemo, 2022). In this geopolitical triangle, China's position has been significantly weakened.

If Trump's administration raised the idea of a complete economic decoupling with China (Reuters, 2020), the Biden administration and his like-minded allies are trying for a partial decoupling. The essence of decoupling is an ultimate negative usage of economic resources by rejecting the rival country's access to markets, key resources, high technologies, and critical human resources. Decoupling is an upgrade of trade war and a typical example of economic warfare.

Although Joe Biden rejects the trade war model vis-à-vis China, the global context is gradually luring the West to adopt an economic warfare approach. It's largely inspired by the West's economic sanctions against Russia and is increasingly used against China, especially in the high-tech areas. The Biden Administration tried to adopt a "small yard, high fence" strategy by creating "choke points" for critical US technologies vis-à-vis China. As Jake Sullivan, Biden's National Security Advisor said, "Foundational technologies have to be inside that yard and the fence has to be high because our strategic competitors should not be able to exploit American and allied technologies to undermine American and allied security (Financial Times, 2022)".

Facing all these challenges, China's economic statecraft had a period of retrenchment, especially during the three years of pandemic (2020–2022). The pandemic isolated China from the rest of the world for three full years, during which the country's BRI projects faced significant challenges. These included difficulties in deploying personnel overseas, supplying materials, and in production activities. Additionally, a substantial portion of China's financial and economic resources was diverted to combat COVID-19.

Confronted with significant risks both domestically and internationally, Xi Jinping remained highly alert. In his speech to the senior government officials in 2019, he cautioned senior officials: "Faced with the unpredictable international situation, the complex and sensitive surrounding environment, and the arduous and heavy tasks of reform, development, and stability, we must always remain highly vigilant. We need to be on high alert for 'black swan' events as well as guard against 'gray rhino' events" (Xi, 2019a).

In another speech, Xi (2019b) elaborated on the risks and emphasized the importance of a combative spirit: "At present and in the coming period, China's development has entered a phase where various risks and challenges are continuously accumulating and even becoming increasingly apparent... Leading officials should possess the ability to discern subtleties and foresee developments, akin to knowing a deer has passed by the rustling of grass and leaves, recognizing the approach of a tiger from the rising pine wind, and perceiving the onset of autumn from the slightest change in a leaf's color. They should have a scientific prediction of potential risks, knowing where the risks lie, what their manifestations are, how they might develop, and engage in struggles when necessary".

Xi Jinping increasingly emphasized economic security. To give a vivid example, when hearing that Contemporary Amperex Technology Co. Limited (CATL) has reached a 37% share in the global power battery market, maintaining the first place globally for six consecutive years, Xi Jinping expressed his mixed feelings with the phrase "both happy and worried". He said, "He is happy that our industry has reached the forefront of the world; his worry is that a sudden surge might initially lead to a boom but ultimately result in a bust. For emerging industries, it is crucial to have well-coordinated planning. It's important to understand the market size, identify the risks, and prevent a situation where one might charge ahead invincibly but end up trapped and completely defeated". Xi further emphasizing that "national industrial policies must be stable and prudent. Formulating and promoting industrial policies should be approached with caution and prudence. Our new energy industry would not only seize opportunities and advance with the trend but also properly balance development and security (Xinhuanet, 2023b)".

Despite these challenges and heightened caution, China continued to advance its economic statecraft initiatives. Xi Jinping introduced three new global initiatives: the Global Security Initiative, the Global Development Initiative, and the Global Civilization Initiative. At the 3rd BRI Forum, both the China Development Bank and the Export-Import Bank of China announced the establishment of a financing window of 350 billion RMB each, cumulatively creating a massive 700 billion RMB (approximately 100 billion USD) financing window. Additionally, an extra 80 billion RMB (approximately 11.8 billion USD) will be injected into the Silk Road Fund (Xinhuanet, 2023a).

In summary, China's economic statecraft initially experienced a phase of optimism during Xi Jinping's first term (2012–2017). However, it faced challenges and a degree of retrenchment during his second term (2017–2022), particularly during the pandemic. Despite these challenges, China's economic statecraft has shown resilience. It is premature to predict a complete retrenchment of China's economic statecraft, and the country possesses vast economic resources that enable it to sustain its initiatives despite increasing resistance and fatigue.

Reference List

Adeyemo, W. (2022) *America's New Sanctions Strategy: How Washington Can Stop the Russian War Machine and Strengthen the International Economic Order* [Foreign Affairs] 16 December. Available at: https://www.foreignaffairs.com/russian-federation/americas-new-sanctions-strategy.

BBC (2021) *China Says US Cannot Speak from 'A Position of Strength'* [BBC] 19 March. Available at: https://www.bbc.com/news/av/world-56456021.

Clinton, H. (2011) *America's Pacific Century* [Foreign Policy] 11 October. Available at: https://foreignpolicy.com/2011/10/11/americas-pacific-century/.

European Commission (2021) *EU Strengthens Protection against Economic Coercion* [European Commission] 8 December. Available at: https://ec.europa.eu/commission/presscorner/detail/en/ip_21_6642.

European Council on Foreign Relations (2022) *The Birth of Geopolitical Europe: In Conversation with Josep Borrell* [European Council on Foreign Relations] 29 March. Available at: https://ecfr.eu/event/the-birth-of-a-geopolitical-europe-in-conversation-with-josep-borrell/.

Financial Times (2022) *Joe Biden Warns US Faces 'Decisive Decade' in Rivalry with China* [Financial Times] 13 October. Available at: https://www.ft.com/content/c9011130-a119-40d5-beb9-a09e7faff2e1.

Lardy, N. (2019) *STATE STRIKES BACK: The End of Economic Reform in China?* S.L: The Peterson Institute Fo.

Leahy, J., Yu, S., and White, E. (2023) *Li Keqiang, Chinese Premier, 1955–2023* [Financial Times] 27 October. Available at: https://www.ft.com/content/a088696e-d696-4f2e-a543-7a5ba1ada1d2.

Lynch, S., and Gridneff, I. (2022) *Europe's American president: The paradox of Ursula von der Leyen* [Politico] 6 October. Available at: https://www.politico.eu/article/europe-american-president-paradox-ursula-von-der-leyen/.

New York Times (2019) *Red Scare Grows in Washington and Now with China as the Boogeyman* [New York Times] 21 July.

People (2015) *The Central Economic Work Conference Proposed to Pay More Attention to Supply-side Structural Reforms* [The State Council of The People's Republic of China] 28 December. Available at: https://www.gov.cn/xinwen/2015-12/28/content_5028343.htm.

People (2021) *A New Chapter on the Righteous Path on Earth (Study Q&A on Xi Jinping's Thought on Socialism with Chinese Characteristics for a New Era IV) – On Adherence to and Development of Socialism with Chinese Characteristics for a New Era* [People] 22 July. Available at: http://politics.people.com.cn/n1/2021/0722/c1001-32165548.html.

People's Daily (2017) *Xi Jingping Had His First Meeting with Trump* [People's Daily] 8 April.

Posen, A. (2019) *Preface in Nicholas R. Lardy's The State Strikes Back: The End of Economic Reform in China?* S.L: The Peterson Institute Fo.

Reuters (2020) *Trump Again Raises Idea of Decoupling Economy from China* [Reuters] 16 September. Available at: https://www.reuters.com/article/usa-trump-china-idUSKBN25Z08U.

Reynolds, M., and Goodman, P. (2022) *China's Economic Coercion: Lessons from Lithuania.* [CSIS] 6 May. Available at: https://www.csis.org/analysis/chinas-economic-coercion-lessons-lithuania.

Shirk, S. (2023) *Overreach: How China Derailed Its Peaceful Rise*. London: Oxford University Press.

The Council of the EU (2020) *EU Adopts a Global Human Rights Sanctions Regime* [European Council] 7 December. Available at: https://www.consilium.europa.eu/en/press/press-releases/2020/12/07/eu-adopts-a-global-human-rights-sanctions-regime/?utm_source=dsms-auto&utm_medium=email&utm_campaign=EU+adopts+a+global+human+rights+sanctions+regime.

The White House. (2022) *Executive Order on the Implementation of the CHIPS Act of 2022* [The White House] 25 August. Available at: https://www.whitehouse.gov/briefing-room/presidential-actions/2022/08/25/executive-order-on-the-implementation-of-the-chips-act-of-2022/.

US State Department Archived Content (2009) *U.S. Support for the New Silk Road* [U.S. Department of State]. Available at: https://2009-2017.state.gov/p/sca/ci/af/newsilkroad/index.htm.

Wang, J. (2012) *"Westward": China's Geostrategic Rebalancing* [Aisixiang] 19 October. Available at: https://www.aisixiang.com/data/58232.html.

World Bank (2023) *GDP Data: China.* Available at: https://data.worldbank.org/indicator/NY.GDP.MKTP.KD.ZG?end=2022&locations=CN&start=2000 (Accessed: December 2, 2023)

Xi, J. P. (2017) *The Governance of China. II*. Beijing, China: Foreign Languages Press.

Xi, J. P. (2018) *Full Text of Chinese President Xi Jinping's Speech at Opening Ceremony of the 2018 Forum on China-Africa Cooperation (FOCAC) Beijing Summit* [China Daily] 4 September. Available at: http://www.chinadaily.com.cn/a/201809/04/WS-5b8d5c25a310add14f389592.html.

Xi, J. P. (2019a) *Speech by President Xi Jinping at the Opening Ceremony of the Seminar for Provincial and Ministerial-level Leading Officials on Adhering to Bottom-line Thinking and Focusing on Preventing and Resolving Major Risks*, 21 January.

Xi, J. P. (2019b) *Speech by President Xi Jinping at the Opening Ceremony of the Training Class for Young and Middle-aged Officials at the Central Party School*, 3 September, Beijing.

Xi, J. P. (2022) *Speech at the Opening Ceremony of the Training Course for Young and Middle-aged Cadres of the Central Party School (National School of Administration) for the Spring Semester of 2022* [Ministry of Education of the People's Republic of China] 1 March. Available at: http://www.moe.gov.cn/jyb_xwfb/moe_176/202306/t20230630_1066550.html.

Xinhuanet (2017) *Xi Jinping Receives Envoys Attending 2017 Annual Conference for Chinese Ambassadors and Consuls Abroad and Delivered an Important Speech Xi Jinping Proposed This Concept at the 2017 Annual Conference for Chinese Ambassadors and Consuls Abroad* [The State Council of The People's Republic of China] 28 December. Available at: https://www.gov.cn/xinwen/2017-12/28/content_5251251.htm.

Xinhuanet (2018) *Xi Jinping: Efforts to Create a New Situation in Great Power Diplomacy with Chinese Characteristics* [Xinhuanet] 23 June. Available at: http://www.xinhuanet.com/politics/2018-06/23/c_1123025806.htm.

Xinhuanet (2023a) *Full Text of Xi Jinping's Keynote Speech at 3rd Belt and Road Forum for International Cooperation* [Xinhuanet] 18 October. Available at: https://english.news.cn/20231018/7bfc16ac51d443c6a7a00ce25c972104/c.html.

Xinhuanet (2023b) *Going on a New Journey of Chinese-Style Modernization–Sidebar on General Secretary Xi Jinping's Visit to Members of the People's Political Consultative Conference (CPPCC) Sector of the Democratic Alliance for the Betterment and Progress of Hong Kong (DAB) and Participation in the Group Meeting* [The State Council of The People's Republic of China] 7 March. Available at: https://www.gov.cn/xinwen/2023-03/07/content_5745127.htm.

Zhang, X. T. (2024) *New Economic Statecraft: China, the United States and the European Union*. London and New York, NY: Routledge, 2024.

Conclusion

The Wealth-Power Dialectic: Fundamental to China's Economic Statecraft

Economic statecraft is the strategy employed by a country to expand its economy and leverage its economic strengths to become a strong nation and maintain that status in international politics (Zhang, 2024, p. 1). At the heart of economic statecraft lies the wealth-power conversion. In practicing this strategy, countries, particularly great powers, often concentrate on converting wealth into power. However, they sometimes overlook the inverse process: converting power back into wealth. This oversight is a symptom of what Paul Kennedy (1987) described as "overstretching" in his book "The Rise and Fall of the Great Powers".

When a country conducts economic statecraft, there are three implicit premises: (1) economic resources are relatively sufficient or even unlimited; (2) economic power is fungible and transformable; and (3) the relationship between wealth and power is harmonious, or at least nonconflicting and noncontradictory. However, these three premises are not always present, and thus, three limiting conditions emerge for the implementation of a country's economic statecraft: (1) economic resources are not sufficient but rather are scarce; (2) economic power may not always be transformable; and (3) wealth and power are in a relationship of unity of opposites. The neglect or underestimation of these three implicit premises is often key to the failure of economic statecraft. Economic statecraft should examine these three implicit premises that previous studies have overlooked, that is, how to achieve economic growth, extract economic resources, and achieve the two-way conversion of wealth and power (Zhang, 2024, pp. 17–18). Here, we posit that a wealth-power dialectic exists in the economic statecraft of any country, and China is no exception.

Xi Jinping's new economic statecraft trajectory vividly exemplifies the wealth-power dialectic. Building on the substantial national wealth accumulated since the 1978 reform and opening-up, Xi began to explore how to convert this national wealth into power, gradually steering toward what is termed "great power economic statecraft". Through flagship initiatives like the Belt and Road Initiative (BRI) and drawing inspiration from Confucius-Mencius philosophy, Xi sought to restore China's historical prestige. The newly formulated "righteousness-benefit concept" is a prominent example of this. While

DOI: 10.4324/9781003270379-7

Xi has made significant strides in advancing China's new economic statecraft, marking a high point in the country's economic diplomacy, his approach has not sufficiently addressed the wealth-generation aspect. Instead, there has been an excessive focus on the power-play dimension, thereby disrupting the delicate balance between wealth and power.

Upon concluding this book and reflecting on its contents, we have identified four major findings to share.

6.1 Three Approaches of China's Economic Statecraft

China's economic statecraft has evolved through three distinct approaches: (1) The approach of Emperor Zhu Di, who initiated Admiral Zheng He's voyages across the Indo-Pacific, symbolizing a period of exploration and maritime prowess. (2) Mao Zedong's approach, rooted in Marxist ideology and intertwined with China's classical history, representing a blend of ideological fervor and historical context. (3) Deng Xiaoping's approach, characterized by a developmentalist philosophy, focusing on economic growth and modernization as the primary drivers of statecraft.

6.1.1 Emperor Zhu Di's Approach to Economic Statecraft

Emperor Zhu Di of China, like several other capable and ambitious Chinese emperors, adeptly utilized a traditional Chinese economic statecraft approach. His primary goal was to convert wealth into power, thereby reinforcing the Tributary System. This strategy was integral to ensuring that China maintained its status as the "Central Kingdom". By doing so, Zhu Di sought to sustain China's cultural and economic influence over the nations within the Tributary System, a key aspect of the country's foreign policy during his reign.

Emperor Zhu Di's approach to economic statecraft was rooted in traditional Chinese philosophy, particularly the teachings of Confucius and Mencius. This strategy emphasized China's economic superiority but did not aim for direct economic gain. Instead, it focused on upholding the "Tianxia system", a China-centric world order. Unlike colonialism, which sought territorial conquest, China's approach aimed to preserve a cultural hierarchy with China at the apex of the Tributary System. A significant challenge in maintaining this system was overextension, exemplified by the cessation of Admiral Zheng He's voyages and the destruction of his travel logs after Zhu Di's death, largely due to internal dissent. The agricultural nature of China's economy, vulnerable to weather and land limitations, made sustaining the Tributary System financially burdensome. For ambitious emperors like Zhu Di (1402–1424 AD), Han Wu (141 BC–87 BC), and Sui Yang (605–618 AD), a key challenge was mobilizing economic resources for military and major statecraft projects, where failure could lead to the dynasty's downfall.

6.1.2 Mao Zedong's Approach to Economic Statecraft

Mao Zedong, a prominent Marxist, adapted the ideology to fit China's unique conditions and historical context. He developed a distinct path of Marxism with Chinese characteristics, avoiding dogmatic adherence to the theory. However, his approach to economic statecraft, which combined Marxism with traditional Chinese methods, placed significant strain on China's economy. Marxism's strengths lay in mobilizing resources for wartime efforts and regime survival, but its planned economic aspects were less effective in fostering long-term economic growth. Mao's hasty efforts to implement Communism resulted in economic and political turmoil, exemplified by the "Great Leap Forward" campaign.

Simultaneously, Mao's perspective was deeply influenced by China's historical context, viewing China as a major nation with responsibilities toward smaller countries. His profound understanding of Chinese history, particularly the strategic importance of Korea across different dynasties, influenced his decision to support Korea, even at the expense of engaging in conflict with UN-allied forces led by the United States. This decision reflected a blend of ideological commitment and historical awareness in Mao's economic and diplomatic strategies. In many ways, Mao Zedong represented China's Marxist economic statecraft with the influence of traditional Chinese history.

Mao Zedong's approach to economic statecraft was a unique blend of Marxist principles, adapted to align with China's specific needs and circumstances, and influenced by the nation's rich traditional history. This synthesis allowed him to craft policies that reflected both the revolutionary ideals of Marxism and the enduring lessons from China's historical experiences.

6.1.3 Deng Xiaoping's Approach to Economic Statecraft

While Deng Xiaoping was a Marxist, his approach to economic statecraft diverged significantly from traditional Marxist doctrines, focusing instead on developmental pragmatism. He maintained respect for Mao Zedong, his predecessor, recognizing Mao's achievements while also addressing his errors. Deng's perspective on world affairs transcended ideological lines, prioritizing pragmatic diplomacy and economic development.

Deng's legacy is most notably marked by his initiation of the reform and opening-up policies and his influential "Southern Tour", which played a crucial role in integrating China into the global market economy. His economic strategies emphasized modernization, integration with international financial institutions, and practical solutions over ideological rigidity.

Deng's focus was on wealth generation rather than its conversion into power. He is known for advocating the principle of "keeping a low profile" and "biding time", contributing to a period of sustained economic growth and relative international peace for China.

Under Deng's guidance, China's economic policy shifted toward a market economy and global engagement. His chosen successors, Jiang Zemin and Hu Jintao, continued to adhere to and expand upon these developmental strategies. Deng Xiaoping's approach to economic statecraft, emphasizing reform, opening-up, and pragmatic engagement with the global economy, is widely regarded as one of the most successful in China's post-1949 history.

6.2 China's Post-1978 Economic Statecraft Model: Marxist-Developmentalist Compromise

The remarkable economic ascent of China since 1978 can be attributed to a unique blend of Marxist ideology and developmentalist economics, a compromise forged within the Communist Party of China (CPC). This compromise maintained Marxism as the dominant ideological framework while simultaneously embracing economic liberalism as the driving force behind China's statecraft.

Jiang Zemin, Deng Xiaoping's handpicked successor, encapsulated this approach with the concept of the Socialist Market Economy. This model symbolizes the Marxist-Developmentalist compromise, representing more of a middle ground between the CPC's left-wing preference for planned economics and the right-wing inclination toward market mechanisms and capitalist elements. The balance struck between Marxist ideology and developmentalist economics has been instrumental in guiding China's development since the initiation of the reform and opening-up policies in 1978. Despite facing challenges, this equilibrium has effectively steered China's rapid economic growth and transformation.

Deng Xiaoping's philosophy, known as the "three favorables", emphasized policies that were favorable to enhancing productivity, national power, and the living standards of the people. This approach was used as a metric to assess whether China's developments aligned with socialist or capitalist principles. Jiang Zemin's "three represents" philosophy highlighted the CPC's representation of the most advanced productivity, culture, and people's interests. Hu Jintao introduced the "Scientific Development Philosophy", while Xi Jinping advocates the "New Development Philosophy", which emphasizes innovation, coordination, green development, openness, and sharing, proposed in October 2015 during the Fifth Plenary Session of the 18th Communist Party of China Central Committee (Qiushi, 2021). These philosophies collectively embody the enduring Marxist-Developmentalist Compromise, crucial to the CPC's long-term governance strategy.

Xi Jinping continues to uphold this compromise, though he faces the complex task of balancing traditional Marxist principles with the realities of economic liberalism. This balancing act is central to understanding the current dynamics of China's economic statecraft and its future trajectory.

6.3 Xi Jinping's Grand Synthesis: Marxist-Developmentalist Statecraft Enlightened by Confucius-Mencius

Xi Jinping's approach to economic statecraft represents a comprehensive synthesis, amalgamating elements from the strategies of historical figures like Emperor Zhu Di, Mao Zedong, and Deng Xiaoping. This approach can be characterized as "Marxist-Developmentalist Statecraft Enlightened by Confucius-Mencius".

Xi Jinping (2022) shows a deep appreciation for Confucius-Mencius philosophy, echoing Confucius's ideal of a gentleman who cultivates himself, manages his household, governs the state, and ultimately brings peace to the world. His focus on "governing the state" is evident in his most significant writings.

Moreover, Xi Jinping demonstrates a profound understanding of the philosophy of history, contemplating the enduring question of overcoming the dynastic cycle of rise and decline – a question also pondered by Mao Zedong. Mao's solution was "public supervision", advocating that government accountability to the people prevents governance lapses. At the 6th Plenary Session of the 19th CPC Central Committee, Xi Jinping offered his own answer: "self-revolution", emphasizing the need to confront internal challenges, maintain the party's progressiveness and purity, and continually enhance its creativity, cohesion, and combat effectiveness (Liu, 2022).

While a committed Marxist, Xi Jinping respects the "Marxist-Developmentalist Compromise" established since Deng Xiaoping's era. Recognizing the importance of economic growth, Xi Jinping was also aware early in his tenure that the era of double-digit economic growth was over, and a "New Normal" of slower growth would be China's reality in the coming decade. The effectiveness of Xi Jinping's approach in addressing the "New Normal" of China's economic statecraft remains an open question, particularly as his second term progresses and beyond.

Ambitious, determined, ideologically driven, and yet pragmatically experienced, Xi Jinping has endeavored to create a grand synthesis, blending Marxist-Developmentalist Statecraft with insights from Confucius-Mencius and Chinese history. This synthesis is reflected in initiatives like the BRI, the "New Righteousness-Benefit Philosophy", and the concept of a "Community of Shared Future for Mankind". Xi Jinping carries a strong sense of historical responsibility and urgency to accomplish significant objectives within his tenure, leading to an ambitious agenda. However, this haste has also led to overextension and stress, impacting both China and the global community.

6.4 Overstretch: The Biggest Challenge to Xi Jinping's Major-Country Economic Statecraft

Xi Jinping's approach to major-country economic statecraft is a natural progression for an ambitious and capable leader, and he has achieved notable success, particularly in enhancing China's international reputation in developing countries. This success has instilled a sense of pride among many Chinese citizens regarding China's elevated global standing. Initiatives like the BRI and the Asian Infrastructure Investment Bank (AIIB) are innovative and aimed at righteous causes.

However, the challenges Xi faces lie primarily in the wealth-power dialectic intrinsic to economic statecraft – a dilemma not unique to China but common among great powers. The cornerstone of successful economic statecraft for any great power is its economic growth. Xi inherited a substantial national wealth accumulated since 1978, allowing him to wield economic power in ways his predecessors could not. Yet, he also faced the challenge of a slowing economy early in his rule, creating tension between his ambitious statecraft agenda and the reality of China's economic slowdown.

As a staunch Marxist, Xi has made significant strides, such as eradicating absolute poverty in China within three years (2018–2020) (Xinhuanet, 2021). However, his strict adherence to Marxist ideology has clashed with capitalist elements in China's economy. His efforts to regulate sectors like the Internet, housing, finance, and even education have led to a decline in private sector confidence. Maintaining the balance between Marxism and economic liberalism has become increasingly challenging in his second term and beyond. The private sector plays a crucial role in China's economic growth, contributing significantly to tax revenue and job creation. A market economy necessitates advanced institutions for effective economic management. Over-reliance on Marxist-style planned economy approaches and excessive state interventions can potentially hinder China's economic growth.

Additionally, Xi's relations with the United States and the West in general have deteriorated, complicating his diplomatic and statecraft efforts. The more adversarial the West's stance toward China, the more Xi has emphasized ideological purity and national security.

This ideological shift under Xi Jinping has prompted a focus on garnering support from the poor and lower working class, a strategy that risks alienating the wealthier and more cosmopolitan upper-middle class. This evolving dynamic poses a challenge to the Marxist-Developmentalist compromise that has been a cornerstone of Chinese leadership over the past four decades. To sustain a developmentalist economic policy, it is essential to preserve key elements of the market economy. Additionally, allowing a degree of economic liberalism is crucial for maintaining public confidence in both the economy and the broader society.

The fundamental challenge for Xi in governing China remains economic. The effectiveness of policies such as the Supply-side Structural Reform, initiated with Premier Li Keqiang, has been limited. The question of what new economic policies or ways of thinking are necessary remains open. Perhaps a reconsideration of Deng Xiaoping's economic liberal pragmatism is needed.

However, the context has significantly changed since Deng's era, and under Xi's leadership, China is navigating uncharted waters.

China's economic and social experiment continues, with its great power economic statecraft under Xi's tenure being a critical and impactful experiment in governance and statecraft, both for China and the global community. It is still too early to predict the failures of China's economic statecraft. Perhaps it would be wiser to consider the global implications should China's great power statecraft fail. China is simply too big to fail, and the world cannot afford its failure.

Reference List

Kennedy, P. (1987) *The Rise and Fall of the Great Powers: Economic Change and Military Conflict from 1500–2000*. New York, NY: Random House.

Liu, X. Z. (2022) *Two Answers: Stepping Outside the Historical Cyclical Rate* [People] 27 January. Available at: http://dangjian.people.com.cn/n1/2022/0127/c117092-32340904.html.

Qiushi (2021) *Xi Jinping: Grasp the New Stage of Development, Implement the New Development Concept and Build a New Development Pattern* [The State Council of The People's Republic of China] 30 April. Available at: https://www.gov.cn/xinwen/2021-04/30/content_5604164.htm.

Xi, J. P. (2022) *The Governance of China. IV*. Beijing, China: Foreign Languages Press.

Xinhuanet (2021) *Xi Jinping: Speech at the National Poverty Eradication Summary and Commendation Ceremony* [Xinhuanet] 25 February. Available at: http://www.xinhuanet.com/politics/leaders/2021-02/25/c_1127140240.htm

Zhang, X. T. (2024) *New Economic Statecraft: China, the United States and the European Union*. London and New York, NY: Routledge.

Index

For Product Safety Concerns and Information please contact our EU representative GPSR@taylorandfrancis.com
Taylor & Francis Verlag GmbH, Kaufingerstraße 24, 80331 München, Germany

www.ingramcontent.com/pod-product-compliance
Lightning Source LLC
LaVergne TN
LVHW021113300926
849160LV00009B/721